Arduino Development Cookbook

Over 50 hands-on recipes to quickly build and
understand Arduino projects, from the simplest
to the most extraordinary

Cornel Amariei

BIRMINGHAM - MUMBAI

Arduino Development Cookbook

First published: April 2015

Production reference: 1170415

Published by Packt Publishing Ltd.
Livery Place
35 Livery Street
Birmingham B3 2PB, UK.

ISBN 978-1-78398-294-3

www.packtpub.com

Cover Image by Cornel Amariei (cornelam@gmail.com)

Credits

Author

Cornel Amariei

Reviewers

Simone Bianchi

Wilson da Rocha França

Vincent Gijsen

Francis Perea

Commissioning Editor

Edward Gordon

Acquisition Editor

Sam Wood

Content Development Editor

Ritika Singh

Technical Editor

Vivek Arora

Copy Editors

Charlotte Carneiro

Puja Lalwani

Project Coordinator

Judie Jose

Proofreaders

Simran Bhogal

Stephen Copestake

Indexer

Rekha Nair

Graphics

Laurentiu Mihailescu

Abhinash Sahu

Production Coordinator

Komal Ramchandani

Cover Work

Komal Ramchandani

About the Author

Cornel Amariei is a Romanian inventor and entrepreneur in the fields of Robotics and 3D printing. He has been working with the Arduino platform since its early days in 2007. His past experience involves large cargo gamma ray scanning robotics, ATM security systems, and blind assisting devices. In his spare time, he is a performing musician playing multiple instruments—predominately the guitar. He is also a swimmer, water polo player, and photographer.

Over the years, he has built hundreds of Arduino projects, ranging from flying Quadcopters to levitating magnets and underwater robots. Currently, he splits his time between doing his undergraduate studies in electric engineering and computer science at Jacobs University in Bremen, Germany, and his start-ups and research and development job.

I would like to thank my parents: my mother, Cristina, and my father, Eugen, for buying me my first technology book 18 years ago. I don't know whether this was the intended path they had in mind for me, but considering the amount of support they offered during the writing of this book, I believe now it is.

I would also like to thank my friends, colleagues, and business partners for accepting my new project and providing me with the time required to complete it, even if this meant more work for them.

Finally, I would like to thank Packt Publishing for offering me the chance to write this book and for handling all the delays I brought to the project, as most of this book was written in transit, short breaks, late nights, and early mornings.

Thank you.

About the Reviewers

Simone Bianchi lives in Italy, where he got a degree in electronic engineering.

Now he works full time for a software house as a Java developer. In his spare time, he likes to feed his curious side by exploring other topics so that he can develop components for the Talend platform, an app for the Android system, delight himself by building IoT projects using different micro controllers (such as the Arduino and Spark Core) with the help of his 6-year-old nephew, Leonardo, or simply learn new things such as AngularJS or 3D graphics.

I'd like to thank Packt Publishing for giving me the opportunity to review their book again after *Talend for Big Data* and *Arduino Android Blueprints*, and I hope I have contributed to making this your favorite book companion during your Arduino projects.

Leo, here is your project book.

Wilson da Rocha França is a system architect in a leading online retail company in Latin America. He is an IT professional, computer science passionate, and an open source enthusiast; he graduated with a university degree from Centro Federal de Educação Tecnológica Celso Suckow da Fonseca, Rio de Janeiro, Brazil, in 2005 and also holds a master of business administration degree from Universidade Federal do Rio de Janeiro in 2010.

He is passionate about e-commerce and the Web; he had the opportunity to work not only in online retail, but also in other markets, such as comparison shopping and online classifieds. He has dedicated most of his time to being a Java web developer.

He is currently working on a MongoDB book and had also worked as a reviewer on *Instant Varnish Cache How-to, Packt Publishing*.

First and foremost, I would like to thank my wife, Christiane, for standing by me. I would also like to express my special gratitude to Packt Publishing for giving me such attention and time. My thanks and appreciation also go to my family and people who have helped me out with their abilities.

Vincent Gijsen is an all-rounder. With a bachelor's in embedded systems and a master's in information science, he has also worked in a big data start-up and is currently working as a security officer and cyber security consultant regarding vital infrastructure. He has been a reviewer on *Storm Blueprints: Patterns for Distributed Real-time Computation, . Packt Publishing*

He has a broad range of interests. In his spare time, he likes to fiddle with lasers, microcontrollers, and other related electronics, hence this review. He hopes you like this book as much as he enjoyed reviewing it.

Francis Perea is a professional education professor at Consejería de Educación de la Junta de Andalucía in Spain with more than 14 years of experience.

He specializes in system administration, web development, and content management systems. In his spare time, he works as a freelancer and collaborates, among others, with ñ multimedia, a little design studio in Córdoba working as a system administrator and main web developer.

He has also collaborated as a technical reviewer for *SketchUp 2013 for Architectural Visualization*, *Arduino Home Automation*, and *Internet of Things with the Arduino Yún*, by Packt Publishing.

When not sitting in front of a computer or tinkering in his workshop, he can be found mountain biking or kitesurfing or as a beekeeper taking care of his hives in Axarquía County, where he lives.

I would like to thank my wife, Salomé, and our three kids, Paula, Álvaro, and Javi, for all the support they give me even when we all are busy. There are no words to express my gratitude.

I would also like to thank my colleagues in ñ multimedia and my students for being patient. The need to be at the level you demand is what keeps me going forward.

www.PacktPub.com

Support files, eBooks, discount offers, and more

For support files and downloads related to your book, please visit www.PacktPub.com.

Did you know that Packt offers eBook versions of every book published, with PDF and ePub files available? You can upgrade to the eBook version at www.PacktPub.com and as a print book customer, you are entitled to a discount on the eBook copy. Get in touch with us at service@packtpub.com for more details.

At www.PacktPub.com, you can also read a collection of free technical articles, sign up for a range of free newsletters and receive exclusive discounts and offers on Packt books and eBooks.

https://www2.packtpub.com/books/subscription/packtlib

Do you need instant solutions to your IT questions? PacktLib is Packt's online digital book library. Here, you can search, access, and read Packt's entire library of books.

Why Subscribe?

- Fully searchable across every book published by Packt
- Copy and paste, print, and bookmark content
- On demand and accessible via a web browser

Free Access for Packt account holders

If you have an account with Packt at www.PacktPub.com, you can use this to access PacktLib today and view 9 entirely free books. Simply use your login credentials for immediate access.

Table of Contents

Preface

The year was 2005 when a few guys from the Interaction Design Institute Ivrea, Italy wanted to create a simple microcontroller board for their students—a board that was more modern, cheaper, and easier to use than the designs available at that moment. And they named it Arduino, after the local bar, which was named after King Arduino.

The initial version was bulky, complicated to connect, and lacked USB, and other features commonly found these days, but the board had potential. Now, Arduino is renowned for its simplicity and ease of use. Children are building projects using Arduino that only 10 years ago would have required engineers.

The whole design is open sourced and clones of the board can be found everywhere in the world. There is no known number of Arduino boards but it is in the range of hundreds of thousands or even more. Everybody can design their own custom implementation of the standard invented in 2005.

Today, Arduino has been to every corner of the planet and even above it. It has fueled other revolutions such as the maker, the open source and 3D printing movements. It is continuously upgraded to be faster and handle more. But what is Arduino?

Arduino is a microcontroller board, designed to connect to electronics and control them. We can write code for the Arduino that will get data from the environment, and make decisions and take actions based on the data. Robots, 3D printers, toys, even toasters may have an Arduino inside, powering up all the interaction.

This book contains recipes that show how to implement key topics of the Arduino, starting from basic interaction with buttons and LEDs, going up to interaction with the Global Positioning System (GPS), making music, or communicating with the Internet. It is intended for programming or electronics enthusiasts who want to combine the best of both worlds to build interactive projects.

What this book covers

Chapter 1, Power on – Arduino Basics, will teach you to connect, install, and transfer the first program to the Arduino board. This chapter covers the basics of how to use the Arduino board, the types of boards, and how to use the Arduino IDE.

Chapter 2, Blinking LEDs, covers one of the basic uses of Arduino, controlling LEDs. Various types and implementations have been covered, RGB LEDs, blinking and fading LEDs, 7-segment displays, or more advanced control techniques.

Chapter 3, Working with Buttons, will show you how to detect and use buttons as a key input method. Several types of buttons have been covered along with solutions to the most common button implementation issues. Also, ways of connecting more buttons than available digital pins have been shown.

Chapter 4, Sensors, covers the most important sensors that can be connected to the Arduino. Probably the most important thing for Arduino is to be able to read as many parameters from the environment as possible. Using sensors, it can read distance, temperature, light intensity, or even global localization.

Chapter 5, Motor Control, will show you how to connect and control multiple types of motors. Making things move is incredibly easy using motors and Arduino. Small and large, brushless and servos motor along with speed and direction control, have all been covered here.

Chapter 6, More Output Devices, talks about getting more out of Arduino. This chapter covers how to control different loads, how to make sound, how to isolate and protect the board, and how to command more outputs.

Chapter 7, Digital *Communication with Arduino*, covers several communication protocols such as UART, I2C, Serial, and Ethernet, to get the most out of the communication interfaces available on Arduino. Arduino can communicate with other boards, computers, and even the Internet.

Chapter 8, Hacking, talks about the small hacks that can help an Arduino design go further. It includes speeding up the PWM, reacting to external interrupts, or even storing data inside the Arduino forever.

Appendix, Electronics – the Basics, covers the basics of electronics, such as breadboards, Ohm's law, and so on.

What you need for this book

In general, for the recipes in this book you will need the following items:

- An Arduino board

▸ A USB cable to connect the Arduino to the computer

▸ A breadboard with a jumper wire kit

▸ A general set of resistors with values between 100 ohm and 10,000 ohm

▸ An assortment of general LEDs

▸ A few push buttons and switches

▸ 1N4148 and 1N4001/1N4007 diodes

Some of the more focused recipes require specific hardware components in order to implement them. This is a list of specific components required per chapter:

Chapter 2, Blinking LEDs:

▸ RGB LED

▸ 7-segment display with at least one digit

▸ Standard multi-segment bar graph

Chapter 3, Working with Buttons:

▸ 4051 or equivalent multiplexer Integrated Circuit (IC)

Chapter 4, Sensors:

▸ 10K or other potentiometer

▸ LM35 or TMP36 temperature sensor Integrated Circuit (IC)

▸ PIR motion sensor

▸ Gas sensors such as the MQ-3, MQ-4, MQ-5, and others in the series

▸ Sharp IR sensor such as the GP2Y0A21YK

▸ Ultrasonic sensor such as the MaxSonar EZ series or similar

▸ Simple accelerometer breakout such as the ADXL335

▸ Standard I2C

▸ Standard GPS receiver with UART communication

▸ 4051 or equivalent multiplexer Integrated Circuit (IC)

Chapter 5, Motor Control:

▸ Small vibrating motor

▸ Standard NPN transistors such as the BC547, 2N3905, or the TIP120

▸ Standard Logic Level N Channel MOSFETs such as the IRF510 or IRF520

▸ Arduino motor shield

▶ Standard RC servo motor

▶ ULN2003 or ULN2004 Darlington Array IC

▶ Small bipolar stepper motor

▶ Brushless motor with suited ESC

Chapter 6, More Output Devices:

▶ 8-ohm small speaker

▶ Standard NPN transistors such as the BC547, 2N3905, or the TIP120

▶ General 5V relay

▶ 1.5–3.0 V battery with wire terminals

▶ General optocoupler/optoisolator such as the TLP621, 4N35, or LTV-816

▶ A 74HC595 shift register

Chapter 7, Digital Communication with Arduino:

▶ Another Arduino board

▶ RF Link Transmitter and Receiver (434/315 Mhz) or equivalent

▶ Arduino compatbile Ethernet Shield

▶ LCD character Display

▶ Arduino compatible SD shield

Chapter 8, Hacking:

▶ A DC motor

▶ A resistor between 220 ohm and 4,700 ohm

▶ A standard NPN transistor (BC547, 2N3904, N2222A, TIP120) or a logic level-compatible MOSFET (IRF510, IRF520)

▶ A standard diode (1N4148, 1N4001, 1N4007)

Who this book is for

If you want to build programming and electronics projects that interact with the environment, this book will offer you dozens of recipes to guide you through all the major applications of the Arduino platform. It is intended for programming or electronics enthusiasts who want to combine the best of both worlds to build interactive projects.

Sections

This book contains the following sections:

Getting ready

This section tells us what to expect in the recipe, and describes how to set up any software or any preliminary settings needed for the recipe.

How to do it...

This section characterizes the steps to be followed for "cooking" the recipe.

How it works...

This section usually consists of a brief and detailed explanation of what happened in the previous section.

There's more...

It consists of additional information about the recipe in order to make the reader more anxious about the recipe.

See also

This section may contain references to the recipe.

Conventions

In this book, you will find a number of styles of text that distinguish between different kinds of information. Here are some examples of these styles, and an explanation of their meaning.

Code words in text, database table names, folder names, filenames, file extensions, pathnames, dummy URLs, user input, and Twitter handles are shown as follows: "In the loop() function, we first print the half Christmas tree."

A block of code is set as follows:

```
if (logFile) {
    logFile.print(val1); // Write first value
    logFile.print(" "); // Write a space
```

```
        logFile.println(val2); // Write second value
        logFile.close(); // close the file
    }
```

New terms and **important words** are shown in bold. Words that you see on the screen, in menus or dialog boxes for example, appear in the text like this: " To easily find information about a card, run the Arduino IDE built-in example found under **File | Examples | SD | CardInfo**."

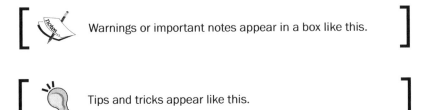

> Warnings or important notes appear in a box like this.

> Tips and tricks appear like this.

Reader feedback

Feedback from our readers is always welcome. Let us know what you think about this book— what you liked or may have disliked. Reader feedback is important for us to develop titles that you really get the most out of.

To send us general feedback, simply send an e-mail to feedback@packtpub.com, and mention the book title via the subject of your message.

If there is a topic that you have expertise in and you are interested in either writing or contributing to a book, see our author guide on www.packtpub.com/authors.

Customer support

Now that you are the proud owner of a Packt book, we have a number of things to help you to get the most from your purchase.

Downloading the example code

You can download the example code files from your account at http://www.packtpub.com for all the Packt Publishing books you have purchased. If you purchased this book elsewhere, you can visit http://www.packtpub.com/support and register to have the files e-mailed directly to you.

Downloading the color images of this book

We also provide you with a PDF file that has color images of the screenshots/diagrams used in this book. The color images will help you better understand the changes in the output. You can download this file from `https://www.packtpub.com/sites/default/files/downloads/2943OS_ColoredImages.pdf`.

Errata

Although we have taken every care to ensure the accuracy of our content, mistakes do happen. If you find a mistake in one of our books—maybe a mistake in the text or the code—we would be grateful if you could report this to us. By doing so, you can save other readers from frustration and help us improve subsequent versions of this book. If you find any errata, please report them by visiting `http://www.packtpub.com/submit-errata`, selecting your book, clicking on the **Errata Submission Form** link, and entering the details of your errata. Once your errata are verified, your submission will be accepted and the errata will be uploaded to our website or added to any list of existing errata under the Errata section of that title.

To view the previously submitted errata, go to `https://www.packtpub.com/books/content/support` and enter the name of the book in the search field. The required information will appear under the **Errata** section.

Piracy

Piracy of copyrighted material on the Internet is an ongoing problem across all media. At Packt, we take the protection of our copyright and licenses very seriously. If you come across any illegal copies of our works in any form on the Internet, please provide us with the location address or website name immediately so that we can pursue a remedy.

Please contact us at `copyright@packtpub.com` with a link to the suspected pirated material.

We appreciate your help in protecting our authors and our ability to bring you valuable content.

Questions

If you have a problem with any aspect of this book, you can contact us at `questions@packtpub.com`, and we will do our best to address the problem.

1
Power on – Arduino Basics

In this chapter, we will cover the following recipes:

- ▸ Downloading the Arduino software
- ▸ Connecting Arduino
- ▸ Uploading code to Arduino
- ▸ Learning Arduino code basics
- ▸ Code basics: Arduino C
- ▸ Code basics: Arduino Pins

Introduction

When we have an idea, we take a pen and we sketch it down on a piece of paper. Imagine if we could build things that interact with the environment just as easily. This is where the Arduino platform comes into play.

Arduino is an open source family of electronic microprocessor boards that we can easily program to understand and interact with the environment. Over the years, Arduino has become the standard for building electronics projects. Arduino has been sent into space to run micro satellites; it has been sent to the bottom of the ocean to control small robotic submersibles; and now, Arduino has arrived for you. Let's explore the limitless world of Arduino.

If you want to go through the basics of electronics before starting with the book, you can refer to the *Appendix, Electronics – the Basics*.

Downloading the Arduino software

The first thing we need is the Arduino **Integrated Development Environment** (**IDE**). One of the best parts about Arduino is that the software in which we need to program the boards is free and open source. The Arduino IDE is compatible with Windows, Mac OS X, and Linux.

Getting ready

We only need one thing to complete this recipe—a computer connected to the Internet.

How to do it...

Follow these simple steps:

1. Visit the Arduino website at `http://arduino.cc/`.
2. In the main menu, go to the **Download** section.
3. Select your operating system and download the latest stable release of the Arduino software. At the time of writing, the latest stable version compatible with all standard boards was version 1.0.5.
4. After it downloads, install the Arduino software.

There's more

Now that we have the Arduino IDE installed, let's familiarize ourselves with the user interface.

Here is a screenshot of the Arduino software running on Windows. It looks the same on Mac and Linux, since it's all written in Java.

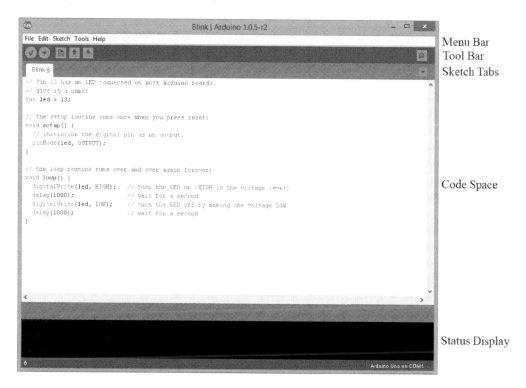

First, we will discuss the Tool Bar. In the Tool Bar, we can find the most used buttons:

Button	Description
	The Verify button compiles the code and checks it for errors.
	The Upload button compiles the code and, if there is no error in the code, uploads it to the Arduino board.
	The New button starts a new program. In the Arduino world, programs are called sketches.
	The Open button simply allows us to open a saved sketch.
	The Save button saves the current sketch.
	This button opens the **Serial Monitor** window that allows us to communicate with the Arduino board. It is extremely helpful when we debug a program. More information can be found in the *Serial output* recipe in *Chapter 7, Digital Communication with Arduino*

In the **Sketch** tab, we can see all the opened Arduino Sketches. This comes handy when we want to work on multiple programs at the same time.

The Code Space area is where all the magic happens. That's where we write the code that powers satellites and cat food dispensers. It's a code editor with automatic syntax highlighting and autoarranging.

The Status Display area indicates all the bad stuff. Whenever there are errors in the code, they will be displayed there. It also displays errors in the connection with the board. The only good thing it can display is that the code has been successfully uploaded to the Arduino board.

Additional functionality can be found in the main menu bar. Here, we have the classic **File** menu where we have **Save**, **Open**, **Close**, and also some examples. In the following recipes, more will be discussed about the menu bar components. A nice trick worth sharing is in the **Tools** menu—the **Auto Format** tool will format the code to look professional and clean.

See also

Consider the following recipes to better understand how to use the Arduino software environment:

- The *Connecting Arduino* recipe
- The *Uploading code to Arduino* recipe

Connecting Arduino

Before we can start writing code and making things move, we first need to connect the Arduino board to our computer. The Arduino board is compatible with Mac, Windows, and Linux. Here we will discuss how to connect and install the drivers.

Getting ready

The following are the ingredients required for this recipe:

- An Arduino board connected to the computer via USB
- The Arduino IDE downloaded and installed

How to do it...

This recipe is split in two, as the steps for Mac and Windows are slightly different.

Mac OS X

Follow these steps to connect Arduino to Mac OS X:

1. Connect the Arduino to the computer using a USB cable. If everything is properly connected, the green light will turn and stay on.

2. If you have an Arduino Uno, Leonardo, Due, or Mega 2560, no drivers are needed and the board is ready to go.

3. If you're using an older Arduino board such as the Duemilanove, Diecimila, or Pro Mini, you will require FTDI drivers. To obtain them, you can visit `http://www.ftdichip.com/Drivers/VCP.htm` and download the latest. After downloading them, click on the installer and follow the instructions. Finally, reboot the computer and the Arduino board will be installed.

Windows

The following steps are required for the Uno, Mega 2560, Leonardo, and Due boards when connecting Arduino to Windows:

1. Connect the Arduino to the computer using a USB cable. If everything is properly connected, the green light will turn on and stay on.

2. Windows will begin its driver installation process and fail. Click the Start button and open the **Control Panel**. There, navigate to **System** and then **Device Manager**.

3. In the **Device Manager** window, search for **Ports (COM & LPT)** and look for a port with a name similar to your board. For the Arduino Uno, the port should be named **Arduino UNO....** If there is no such title under **Ports**, look in **Other Devices** for an **Unknown Device**. That will be your Arduino board.

4. Right-click on the Arduino Board in **Device Manager** and choose **Update Driver Software**. Next, **select Browse my computer for driver software**.

5. This will require the path to the Arduino driver. This can be found in the `Arduino` installation folder in `Program Files`, in the `drivers` folder. It is named `Arduino.inf`. Select the file and Windows will finish installing the driver.

These are the steps for the older FTDI-based Duemilanove, Diecimila, Nano, and Mega boards:

1. Connect the Arduino to the computer using a USB cable. The green light will turn on if everything is connected properly.

2. In Windows Vista and higher, the drivers will install automatically and the board will be ready for use.

3. If the driver installation fails, navigate to **Device Manager** in a similar fashion as for the newer boards and, under **Ports (COM & LPT)**, search for a **USB Serial Converter** or similar. Choose **Update Driver Software**, select **Browse my computer for driver software**, and then select the `FTDI` driver folder from the `Arduino` installation folder, in the `drivers` folder. After selection, click on **Next** and Windows will finish installing the Arduino board.

See also

The procedure for an Ubuntu Linux computer is at `http://playground.arduino.cc/Linux/Ubuntu`.

Uploading code to Arduino

It's time to power on the Arduino board and make it do something. In this recipe, we will connect the Arduino to the computer and upload an example sketch from the Arduino IDE.

Getting ready

To execute this recipe, the following are the components required:

▶ A computer with the Arduino IDE installed

▶ An Arduino board connected to the computer via USB

How to do it...

Follow these steps:

1. Connect the Arduino to the computer using a USB cable. If everything is properly connected, the green LED light will turn on.

2. If this is the first time the Arduino has been connected to the computer, driver installation might be required. Please follow the *Connecting Arduino* recipe to properly set up the Arduino board.

3. Start the Arduino IDE and, in the Menu Bar, go to **File | Examples | 01. Basics** and click on the **Blink** example. This will load the **Blink** sketch.

4. Make sure your Arduino board is selected in the **Board** menu. The menu can be found in the Menu bar in **Tools | Board**.

5. We need to check whether the correct serial port is selected. Under **Tools | Serial Port**, we can see all available serial port devices connected to the computer. On Windows, each port will be labeled as COM followed by a number. Usually, Arduino installs on COM3, but not always. A fast way to check which serial port the Arduino is connected to is to unplug the cable and see which COM port disappears in the menu. That will be our Arduino board. In the Mac, the port should be called something beginning with `/dev/tty.usbmodem` or `/dev/tty.usbserial`.

6. Click on the Upload button on the Tool Bar. If everything runs properly, the TX RX LEDs on the Arduino board will begin blinking for a short time until the upload is done. After this, one LED light on the Arduino Board should slowly blink.

How it works...

When we upload a sketch to the board, the Arduino software first compiles the code. If there is an error in the code, it will write it in the Status Display area and will stop the upload. If no errors are found, it will begin writing the compiled code to the board. Errors will appear if the board or serial port is not properly selected. When everything is correctly set up, the TX RX LEDs will blink, meaning data is being transferred between the computer and the Arduino board. When the transfer is done, the board will reset and the code will immediately begin executing.

The code is stored in the Arduino board until it is erased or replaced by another code. We can take the board and plug it into a battery or to another computer, and it will still execute this blinking.

Learning Arduino code basics

Here we begin with the basics of coding for Arduino. Writing code for Arduino and other embedded platforms is a little different from writing code for a computer. But don't fear—the differences are small.

Getting ready

To execute this recipe, we need just one ingredient: the Arduino IDE running on a computer.

How to do it...

These are the two mandatory functions in the Arduino coding environment:

```
void setup() {
  // Only execute once when the Arduino boots
}


void loop(){
  // Code executes top-down and repeats continuously
}
```

How it works...

Each Arduino sketch has two mandatory functions: the `setup()` function and the `loop()` function. The `setup()` function only executes once: either when we apply power to the Arduino or when it resets. Usually, we use this function to configure the pins of the Arduino, to start communication protocols, such as serial communication, or to perform actions we only want to perform once when the Arduino boots.

The `loop()` function executes continuously. Code in this function is executed top-down; when it reaches the end of the function, it jumps back to the start and runs again. This happens forever until the Arduino is switched off. In here, we write the code we want to run continuously.

See also

Continue the Arduino code basics with the following recipe, *Code basics: Arduino C*.

Code basics – Arduino C

The Arduino uses a slightly reduced C/C++ programming language. In this recipe, we will remember a few basics of C/C++.

Getting ready

Ensure that you have the Arduino IDE running on a computer.

How to do it...

Here is a simple example of basic Arduino C/C++ manipulating two variables:

```
// Global Variables
int var1 = 10;
int var2 = 20;

void setup() {
  // Only execute once when the Arduino boots
  var2 = 5; // var2 becomes 5 once the Arduino boots
}


void loop(){
  // Code executes top-down and repeats continuously
  if (var1 > var2){ // If var1 is greater than var2
    var2++; // Increment var2 by 1
  } else { // If var1 is NOT greater than var2
    var2 = 0; // var2 becomes 0
  }
}
```

How it works...

The code plays with two integer variables. Here we have a code breakdown to better explain each step.

First, we declared two global variables—var1 and var2—and we set them to the values of 10 and 20 respectively.

```
// Global Variables
int var1 = 10;
int var2 = 20;
```

When the Arduino boots, it first allocates the global variables into memory. In the setup() function, we change the value of var2 to 5:

```
void setup() {
  // Only execute once when the Arduino boots
  var2 = 5; // var2 becomes 5 once the Arduino boots
}
```

After the Arduino allocates the global variables, it executes the code inside the setup() function once. Following this, the loop() function will execute repeatedly. Inside, we have an if condition that will play with the values of var2. If var1 is greater than var2, we increase var2 by one. Eventually, var1 will not be greater than var2, and then we set var2 to 0. This will result in an infinite adding and equaling of var2.

This is one example on how the Arduino executes the code in its two main functions.

See also

Continue the Arduino code basics with the following recipe, *Code basics – Arduino pins*.

Code basics – Arduino pins

The most important feature of the Arduino is its control over digital **input/output (I/O)** pins. On each pin, we can set a voltage value of 5 V, representing logic HIGH, or 0 V, representing logic LOW. Also, we can read whether a value of 5 V or 0 V is applied externally. Here we will learn how.

Getting ready

For this recipe, ensure that you have the Arduino IDE running on a computer.

How to do it...

The following code turns a pin HIGH and LOW repeatedly while reading the external voltage applied to another:

```
void setup() {
    // Set pin 2 as a digital Output
    pinMode(2, OUTPUT);
    // Set pin 3 as a digital Input
    pinMode(3, INPUT);
}

void loop(){

    // Set pin 2 HIGH
    digitalWrite(2, HIGH);
    // Wait 100 milliseconds
    delay(100);
    // Set pin 2 LOW
    digitalWrite(2, LOW);
    // Wait 100 milliseconds
    delay(100);

    // Read the value of pin 3 and store it in a variable
    int pinValue = digitalRead(3);
}
```

How it works...

The code sets two pins in output and input mode and then writes and reads from them. Here is the code breakdown:

In setup(), we use the pinMode() function to set pin number 2 as an output. When we set a pin as an output, we can set that pin as either HIGH (5 V) or LOW (0 V). Also, we set pin number 3 as an input. A pin configured as input can read external voltages applied to it. It can read HIGH if the voltage is around 5 V and LOW if the voltage is close or equal to 0 V:

```
void setup() {
    // Set pin 2 as a digital Output
```

```
   pinMode(2, OUTPUT);
   // Set pin 3 as a digital Input
   pinMode(3, INPUT);
}
```

In the `loop()` function, we use the `digitalWrite()` function to set pin number 2 to HIGH. Then, we wait for 100 milliseconds using the `delay()` function. This function stops the execution of the code for the specified time, in milliseconds. Thereafter, we set the pin to LOW and wait another 100 milliseconds. In the end, we read the value of pin 3 in a variable:

```
void loop(){

  // Set pin 2 HIGH
  digitalWrite(2, HIGH);
  // Wait 100 milliseconds
  delay(100);
  // Set pin 2 LOW
  digitalWrite(2, LOW);
  // Wait 100 milliseconds
  delay(100);

  // Read the value of pin 3 and store it in a variable
  int pinValue = digitalRead(3);
}
```

Downloading the example code

You can download the example code files from your account at http://www.packtpub.com for all the Packt Publishing books you have purchased. If you purchased this book elsewhere, you can visit http://www.packtpub.com/support and register to have the files e-mailed directly to you.

2
Blinking LEDs

In this chapter, we will cover the following recipes:

- ▸ Blinking LED without delay()
- ▸ Connecting an external LED
- ▸ Fading the external LED
- ▸ RGB LED
- ▸ LED bar graph
- ▸ The 7-segment display

Introduction

In this chapter, we will explore LEDs with the Arduino. The fastest way to get some feedback from a system or from the Arduino is via an LED. They are simple devices which are either on or off. However, they form the basis for advanced technologies such as LED TVs, projectors, or lasers. In this chapter, we will also see how to use them efficiently and explore some interesting applications for them.

LED stands for **Light Emitting Diode** and, in its core, it's just a diode that emits light. LEDs are incredibly common these days and can be found at any common electronics shop. Radioshack, Digikey, Farnell, Sparkfun, Adafruit, or Pololu are just a few places we can buy LEDs from, online.

Blinking LED without delay()

It is easy to make the LED blink on an Arduino. We turn it on, wait, turn it off, wait again, and then we repeat the cycle. However, this wait state will completely halt the Arduino execution. We want to make the LED blink while the Arduino is performing other actions.

Getting ready

For this recipe all you need is an Arduino board connected to the computer via USB.

How to do it...

The following code will make the internal LED blink on the Arduino without ever using the `delay()` function:

```
// Variable for keeping the previous LED state
int previousLEDstate = LOW;

unsigned long lastTime = 0; // Last time the LED changed state
int interval = 200; // interval between the blinks in milliseconds

void setup() {
  // Declare the pin for the LED as Output
  pinMode(LED_BUILTIN, OUTPUT);
}

void loop(){

  // Here we can write any code we want to execute continuously
  // Read the current time
  unsigned long currentTime = millis();

  // Compare the current time with the last time
  if (currentTime - lastTime >= interval){

    // First we set the previous time to the current time
    lastTime = currentTime;

    // Then we inverse the state of the LED
    if (previousLEDstate == HIGH) {
      digitalWrite(LED_BUILTIN, LOW);
      previousLEDstate = LOW;
    } else {
      digitalWrite(LED_BUILTIN, HIGH);
      previousLEDstate = HIGH;
    }
  }
}
```

While most Arduinos have the LED on pin 13, some don't. To make sure we are addressing the correct LED pin, we can use the `LED_BUILTIN` constant. This is already defined in the Arduino language and will always equal the LED pin number of the Arduino board that has been used.

How it works...

The big difference between a normal LED blinking program and this one is that we don't use the `delay()` function. The `delay()` function simply stops the code execution until the specified amount of time passes. Here, we track the internal time of the Arduino; when enough time passes, we change state. The internal time since the start of the Arduino is accessible using the `millis()` function, which will return the time—in milliseconds—since the program started working.

This approach is called non-blocking, since it doesn't block the execution of our code. The `delay()` function is considered to be a blocking function, as it blocks code execution.

Breaking down the code

The code tracks the amount of time passed and changes the state of the LED if enough time has passed.

We need a few variables. The `previousLEDstate` variable will store the last state of the LED. The `lastTime` variable remembers when the LED state changed from `HIGH` to `LOW` or from `LOW` to `HIGH`. When we set a pin as `HIGH`, it will output 5 V. When we set it as `LOW`, it will just go to 0 V.

The `interval` variable is the interval in milliseconds at which we want the LED to change state.

```
// Variable for keeping the previous LED state
int previousLEDstate = LOW;

unsigned long lastTime = 0; // Last time the LED changed state
int interval = 200; // interval between the blinks in milliseconds
```

In the `setup()` function, we set the LED pin as an output:

```
void setup() {
  // Declare the pin for the LED as Output
  pinMode(LED_BUILTIN, OUTPUT);
}
```

The important part comes in the `loop()` function. The first step is to record the time since the Arduino began running the program. The `millis()` function returns very big numbers; variables getting data from this function should always be declared as long or unsigned long. Unsigned variables can only take positive values, from 0 to the maximum allocated space. For example, a normal long variable can take values from -2,147,483,648 up to 2,147,483,648, while an unsigned long can go from 0 up to 4,294,967,295.

```
unsigned long currentTime = millis();
```

Now, we need to see if enough time has passed since the last time we changed the state of the LED. For this, we compare with the previous time. If the difference between the current time and the last is bigger than the interval we declared, we can proceed to change the state of the LED:

```
if (currentTime - lastTime >= interval)
```

When the interval has passed, we first record the new time as being the previous time. By doing this, we reset the time to which we will compare the next time. Then, we check what the previous LED state was and we set the LED to the opposite state. If it was LOW we set it to HIGH and if it was HIGH, we set it to LOW. The previous LED state variable is also set to the new LED state:

```
lastTime = currentTime;

    // Then we inverse the state of the LED
    if (previousLEDstate == HIGH) {
      digitalWrite(LED, LOW);
      previousLEDstate = LOW;
    } else {
      digitalWrite(LED, HIGH);
      previousLEDstate = HIGH;
    }
```

See also

The *Button debouncing* recipe in *Chapter 3, Working with Buttons*, for other topics which avoid the `delay()` function

Connecting an external LED

Luckily, the Arduino boards come with an internal LED connected to pin 13. It is simple to use and always there. But most times we want our own LEDs in different places of our system. We might connect something on top of the Arduino board and can no longer see the internal LED. Here, we will explore how to connect an external LED.

Getting ready

For this recipe, we need the following ingredients:

- An Arduino board connected to the computer via USB
- A breadboard and jumper wires
- A regular LED (the typical LED size is 3 mm)
- A resistor between 220–1,000 ohm

How to do it...

Follow these steps to connect an external LED to an Arduino board:

1. Mount the resistor on the breadboard. Connect one end of the resistor to a digital pin on the Arduino board using a jumper wire.

2. Mount the LED on the breadboard. Connect the anode (+) pin of the LED to the available pin on the resistor. We can determine the anode on the LED in two ways. Usually, the longer pin is the anode. Another way is to look for the flat edge on the outer casing of the LED. The pin next to the flat edge is the cathode (-).

3. Connect the LED cathode (-) to the Arduino GND using jumper wires.

Schematic

This is one possible implementation on the second digital pin. Other digital pins can also be used.

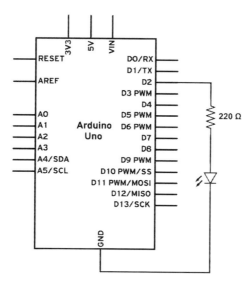

Here is a simple way of wiring the LED:

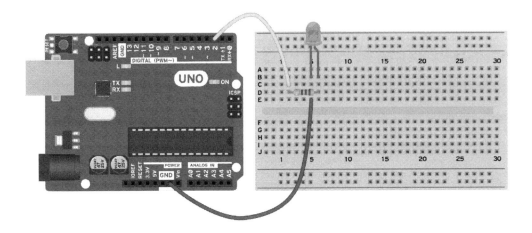

Code

The following code will make the external LED blink:

```
// Declare the LED pin
int LED = 2;

void setup() {
  // Declare the pin for the LED as Output
  pinMode(LED, OUTPUT);
}

void loop(){
  // Here we will turn the LED ON and wait 200 milliseconds
  digitalWrite(LED, HIGH);
  delay(200);
  // Here we will turn the LED OFF and wait 200 milliseconds
  digitalWrite(LED, LOW);
  delay(200);
}
```

 If the LED is connected to a different pin, simply change the LED value to the value of the pin that has been used.

How it works...

This is all semiconductor magic. When the second digital pin is set to `HIGH`, the Arduino provides 5 V of electricity, which travels through the resistor to the LED and GND. When enough voltage and current is present, the LED will light up. The resistor limits the amount of current passing through the LED. Without it, it is possible that the LED (or worse, the Arduino pin) will burn. Try to avoid using LEDs without resistors; this can easily destroy the LED or even your Arduino.

Code breakdown

The code simply turns the LED on, waits, and then turns it off again. Compared to the previous recipe, in this one we will use a blocking approach by using the `delay()` function. Here we declare the LED pin on digital pin 2:

```
int LED = 2;
```

In the `setup()` function we set the LED pin as an output:

```
void setup() {
  pinMode(LED, OUTPUT);
}
```

In the `loop()` function, we continuously turn the LED on, wait 200 milliseconds, and then we turn it off. After turning it off we need to wait another 200 milliseconds, otherwise it will instantaneously turn on again and we will only see a permanently on LED.

```
void loop(){
  // Here we will turn the LED ON and wait 200 miliseconds
  digitalWrite(LED, HIGH);
  delay(200);
  // Here we will turn the LED OFF and wait 200 miliseconds
  digitalWrite(LED, LOW);
  delay(200);
}
```

There's more...

There are a few more things we can do. For example, what if we want more LEDs? Do we really need to mount the resistor first and then the LED?

LED resistor

We do need the resistor connected to the LED; otherwise there is a chance that the LED or the Arduino pin will burn. However, we can also mount the LED first and then the resistor. This means we will connect the Arduino digital pin to the anode (+) and the resistor between the LED cathode (-) and GND. Check the *Diodes and LEDs* recipe in the *Appendix, Electronics – the Basics*, where we discuss the needed resistances to power up an LED. Or, if we want a quick cheat, check the following *See also* section.

Multiple LEDs

Each LED will require its own resistor and digital pin. For example, we can mount one LED on pin 2 and one on pin 3 and individually control each. What if we want multiple LEDs on the same pin? Due to the low voltage of the Arduino, we cannot really mount more than three LEDs on a single pin. For this we require a small resistor, 220 ohm for example, and we need to mount the LEDs in series. This means that the cathode (-) of the first LED will be mounted to the anode (+) of the second LED, and the cathode (-) of the second LED will be connected to the GND. The resistor can be placed anywhere in the path from the digital pin to the GND.

See also

For more information on external LEDs, take a look at the following recipes and links:

- The *Fading the external LED* recipe
- The *RGB LED* recipe
- For more details about LEDs in general, visit `http://electronicsclub.info/leds.htm`
- To connect multiple LEDs to a single pin, read the instructable at `http://www.instructables.com/id/How-to-make-a-string-of-LEDs-in-parallel-for-ardu/`
- Because we are always lazy and we don't want to compute the needed resistor values, use the calculator at `http://www.evilmadscientist.com/2009/wallet-size-led-resistance-calculator/`

Fading the external LED

The LED has two states: ON and OFF. But what if we want to adjust the brightness? How can we do that if we can only turn it ON or OFF? By turning it ON and OFF quickly.

We will use a technique called **Pulse Width Modulation (PWM)**, which is built into the Arduino. It allows us to dim the LED with up to 256 settings.

Getting ready

We require the following ingredients for this recipe:

- ▶ An Arduino board connected to the computer via USB
- ▶ A breadboard and jumper wires
- ▶ A regular LED
- ▶ A resistor between 220–1,000 ohm

How to do it...

This recipe uses the same circuit as the *Connecting an external LED* recipe with a single difference, the pin used to connect the LED is not digital pin 2 but PWM pin 3.

Schematic

This is one possible implementation on the third digital pin. Other digital pins with PWM can be used. On the typical Arduino, such as UNO, there are six pins that also have PWM functionality. These pins are **3**, **5**, **6**, **9**, **10**, and **11**.

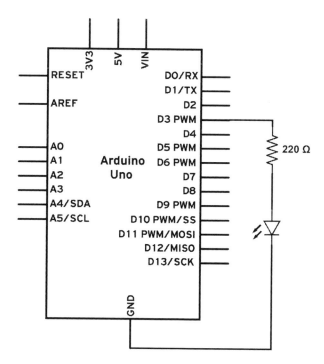

Here is a simple way of wiring the LED:

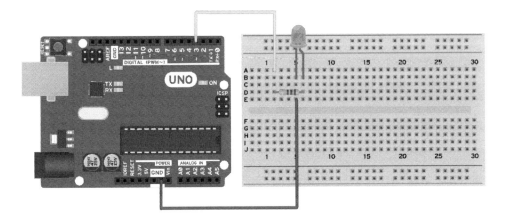

Code

The following code will make the external LED fade:

```
// Declare the LED pin with PWM
int LED = 3;

void setup() {
  // Declare the pin for the LED as Output
  pinMode(LED, OUTPUT);
}

void loop(){
  // Here we will fade the LED from 0 to maximum, 255
  for (int i = 0; i < 256; i++){
    analogWrite(LED, i);
    delay(5);
  }
  // Fade the LED from maximum to 0
  for (int i = 255; i >= 0; i--){
    analogWrite(LED, i);
    delay(5);
  }
}
```

If the LED is connected on a different PWM pin, simply change the LED value to the value of the pin that has been used.

How it works...

This all works with PWM, which works by switching between LOW and HIGH very fast. If we turn a digital pin on and off a thousand times per second, we will obtain, on average, a voltage that is half of the HIGH voltage. If the ratio between HIGH and LOW is 2:3, the obtained voltage will be two-thirds of the HIGH voltage and so on. The following diagram better explains how PWM works:

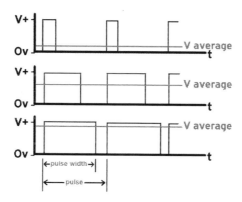

PWM is quite difficult to obtain but, luckily, Arduino has an in-built function that configures all the registers and timers in order to obtain PWM.

Code breakdown

The code fades the LED on and off by changing the PWM. Here, we declare the LED pin on digital pin 3:

```
int LED = 3;
```

In the `setup()` function, we set the LED pin as an output:

```
void setup() {
  // Declare the pin for the LED as Output
  pinMode(LED, OUTPUT);
}
```

In the `loop()` function, we use the important PWM function `analogWrite()`. This function provides an analog signal on the digital PWM pin. The values for the voltage can be between 0–255, 0 for 0 volts and 255 for 5 V or 3.3 V, depending on the Arduino board used. Here, we fade in the LED slowly using a `for` function and then we fade it out:

```
void loop(){
  // Here we will fade the LED from 0 to maximum, 255
  for (int i = 0; i < 256; i++){
    analogWrite(LED, i);
    delay(5);
  }
  // Fade the LED from maximum to 0
  for (int i = 255; i >= 0; i--){
    analogWrite(LED, i);
    delay(5);
  }
}
```

There's more...

The PWM technique is used in almost all digital systems. Sound is digitally produced using this technique; that's how we can listen to music on a computer. Arduino only has a few pins for PWM. They are usually labeled with a ~ sign. The `analogWrite()` function will not work on non-PWM pins.

See also

For more information on PWM, take a look at the following recipes and links:

- ▶ The *RGB LED* recipe
- ▶ http://makezine.com/2011/06/01/circuit-skills-pwm-pulse-width-modulation-sponsored-by-jameco-electronics/

RGB LED

We can get LEDs in a variety of colors these days, but what about an LED that can change color? We all know that a combination of **Red, Green, and Blue** (**RGB**) can give us any color. Using the Arduino PWM functionality, we will see how we can obtain 16 million color combinations with an RGB LED.

RGB LED stands for **Red Green Blue LED**. Inside such an LED we can find one red, one green, and one blue LED, mounted together.

Getting ready

The following are the ingredients needed for this recipe:

- An Arduino board connected to the computer via USB
- A breadboard and jumper wires
- An RGB LED
- Three equal resistors between 220–1,000 ohm

How to do it...

Follow these steps in order to connect an RGB LED to an Arduino board:

1. Mount the RGB LED on the breadboard.
2. We need to identify which pin represents which color and which pin is the common one. The following graphic explains just that:

R C B G

3. Connect **5V** to the common anode (+) of the RGB LED. This is the longest of the four pins.
4. Connect each smaller cathode (-) pin to one individual resistor.
5. Connect each remaining pin on each resistor to an individual PWM pin on the Arduino.

Some RGB LEDs are a common cathode (-) configuration. In this case, connect the cathode (-) to GND.

Schematic

This is one possible implementation using a common anode (+) RGB LED on the PWM, pins **9**, **10**, and **11**:

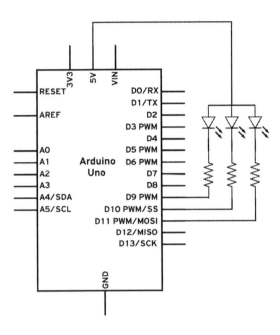

Here is one way of wiring everything on the breadboard:

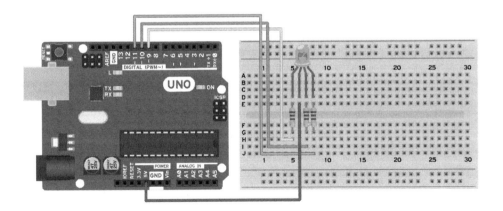

Code

The following code will make the RGB LED change a few colors:

```
// Declare the PWM LED pins
int redLED = 9;
int greenLED = 10;
int blueLED = 11;

void setup() {
  // Declare the pins for the LED as Output
  pinMode(redLED, OUTPUT);
  pinMode(greenLED, OUTPUT);
  pinMode(blueLED, OUTPUT);
}

// A simple function to set the level for each color from 0 to 255
void setColor(int redValue, int greenValue, int blueValue){
  analogWrite(redLED, 255 - redValue);
  analogWrite(greenLED, 255 - greenValue);
  analogWrite(blueLED, 255 - blueValue);
}
void loop(){
  // Change a few colors

  setColor(255, 0, 0); // Red Color
  delay(500);

  setColor(0, 255, 0); // Green Color
  delay(500);

  setColor(0, 0, 255); // Blue Color
  delay(500);

  setColor(255, 255, 0); // Yellow
  delay(500);

  setColor(0, 255, 255); // Cyan
  delay(500);

  setColor(255, 0, 255); // Magenta
```

```
        delay(500);

        setColor(255, 255, 255); // White
        delay(500);
    }
```

 If the RGB LED is connected to different PWM pins, simply change the values of redLED, greenLED, and blueLED to the values of the pins that have been used.

How it works...

RGB LEDs are made up of three LEDs: one red, one green, and one blue. Because they are physically close together, if we manipulate them individually, the color we will see is the resulting combination of the three LED colors.

Code breakdown

The code controls three LEDs individually using the same technique from the *Fading the External LED* recipe. Here, we declare the three LED pins on the PWM channels 9, 10, and 11:

```
    int redLED = 9;
    int greenLED = 10;
    int blueLED = 11;
```

In the setup() function, we set the LED pins as outputs:

```
    void setup() {
      // Declare the pins for the LED as Output
      pinMode(redLED, OUTPUT);
      pinMode(greenLED, OUTPUT);
      pinMode(blueLED, OUTPUT);
    }
```

Here is a custom function called setColor() that makes everything easier. The function has three parameters and the power for each R, G, and B LED. The values can vary from 0–255 for each LED, which means we have 16,581,375 possible colors. In reality, we will never use that many.

```
    void setColor(int redValue, int greenValue, int blueValue){
      analogWrite(redLED, 255 - redValue);
```

```
    analogWrite(greenLED, 255 - greenValue);
    analogWrite(blueLED, 255 - blueValue);
}
```

 In this example, we use a common anode (+) RGB LED. This means that we control the current that goes into the Arduino pin—and not out—as we usually do. Code-wise in this configuration, when we turn the pin to HIGH or to 255, the LED will be OFF. This is the reason for the `255 - redValue` parameter; it inverts the value.

We use the `loop()` function we created to obtain a few combinations. Here, we only use either full power (255) or 0. We can experiment with in-between values to obtain different colors. Give it a try with this code:

```
void loop(){
  setColor(255, 255, 0); // Yellow
  delay(500);

  setColor(0, 255, 255); // Cyan
  delay(500);

  setColor(255, 0, 255); // Magenta
  delay(500);
}
```

There's more...

There are many types of RGB LEDs. Large displays that we find in concerts or on commercial boards have thousands of RGB LEDs to show the image. There are also many more ways of connecting them.

Common anode (+) or common cathode (-)

An RGB LED has three LEDs within, with one pin tied together. In a common anode (+) version, we will have three LEDs with their anodes (+) connected together. The same holds true for a common cathode (-) configuration, only that the cathode (-) is tied together amongst the LEDs. Common cathodes are easier to use but harder to find.

For a common cathode (-), we connect the cathode to the GND and the three individual anodes to an individual digital pin on the Arduino using resistors.

Without PWM

We don't always need 16 million colors. Simply use the `digitalWrite()` functions and we can still obtain seven colors from the LED.

LED bar graph

We all hate progress bars! They are always delaying us from doing something. But in the Arduino world they can be very handy. Here, we will see how to build one with LEDs. An LED bar graph is just a bunch of LEDs put together in a fancy case, but there are many uses for it. We can display the date from a sensor, show a critical condition, or make a funny light show with it.

Getting ready

We will need the following ingredients to execute this recipe:

- An Arduino board connected to the computer via USB
- A breadboard and jumper wires
- An LED bar graph
- Resistors between 220–1,000 ohm

How to do it...

Following are the steps to connect a 10-segment bar graph to the Arduino:

1. Mount the LED bar graph onto the breadboard.
2. If the bar graph is a common anode (+) configuration, connect the common anode (+) pin to the **5V** port on the Arduino. If the bar graph is a common cathode (-), connect the pin to the **GND** port on the Arduino.
3. Connect each individual segment pin to one individual Arduino digital pin, using a resistor. To make things simple, connect all the segment pins to successive digital pins on the Arduino.

Schematic

This is one possible implementation of a common anode (+) 10-segment LED bar graph:

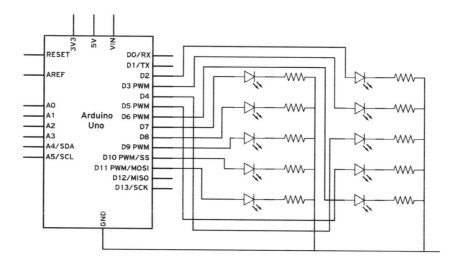

Here is one possible way of wiring it on a breadboard:

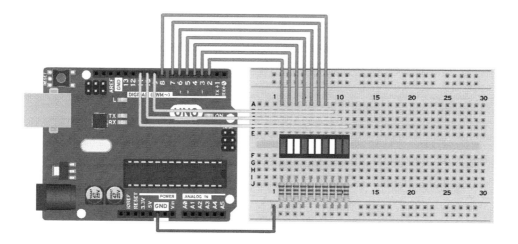

Code

The following code will make the LED bar graph full and then empty:

```
// Declare the first and last Pin of the LED Bar
int pin1 = 2;
int pin10 = 11;

void setup() {
  // Declare the pins as Outputs
  for (int i = pin1; i <= pin10; i++){
    pinMode(i, OUTPUT);
  }
}

// A simple function to set the value of the LED Bar
void setBarValue(int value){
  // First we turn everything off
  for (int i = pin1; i <= pin10; i++){
    digitalWrite(i, HIGH);
  }

  // Write the value we want
  for (int i = pin1; i <= pin1 + value; i++){
    digitalWrite(i, LOW);
  }

  // In case we have value 0
  if (value == 0){
  digitalWrite(pin1, HIGH);
  }
}

void loop(){
  // Play with a few displays

  // Ping-Pong
  for (int i = 0; i <= 10; i++){
    setBarValue(i);
    delay(100);
  }
  for (int i = 10; i >= 0; i--){
    setBarValue(i);
    delay(100);
  }
}
```

This was designed for a common anode (+) configuration. For a common cathode (-) configuration, we need to change the `digitalWrite` function to output the reverse. If it is HIGH, it should output LOW.

How it works...

An LED bar graph is assembled from multiple LEDs. We can control each LED individually to obtain the desired effect. Take a look at the *Connecting an external LED* recipe for more details on external LEDs. In this example, we will write a function to set the progress value on the LED bar graph.

Code breakdown

This code loads and unloads the LED bar graph just like a progress bar. Here, we declare the first and the last pins used in the LED bar. There is no point in declaring all of them as we know they are consecutive in this implementation:

```
int pin1 = 2;
int pin10 = 11;
```

In the `setup()` function, we set each LED pin as an output. This simple trick, used here, helps to set all the pins between `pin1` and `pin10` as outputs:

```
void setup() {
  // Declare the pins as Outputs
  for (int i = pin1; i <= pin10; i++){
    pinMode(i, OUTPUT);
  }
}
```

In the custom `setBarValue()` function, we make the bar show a certain progress level. As the maximum is 10 and the minimum is 0, if we write 5, half the LEDs on the bar will be on while the other half are off:

```
// A simple function to set the value of the LED Bar
void setBarValue(int value){
  // First we turn everything off
  for (int i = pin1; i <= pin10; i++){
    digitalWrite(i, HIGH);
  }

  // Write the value we want
  for (int i = pin1; i <= pin1 + value; i++){
```

```
        digitalWrite(i, LOW);
    }

    // In case we have value 0
    if (value == 0) digitalWrite(pin1, HIGH);
}
```

Finally, in the `loop()` function, we use our custom function to load the bar and then unload it. In the following code, we use a `for` loop to increase the bar value to the maximum and then we decrease it back to 0:

```
void loop(){
    for (int i = 0; i <= 10; i++){
        setBarValue(i);
        delay(100);
    }
    for (int i = 10; i >= 0; i--){
        setBarValue(i);
        delay(100);
    }
}
```

There's more...

LED bar graphs can be very helpful in various situations. Usually they are used to show the battery level on a system or the value of a sensor. A few variations on the bar can be seen as follows.

Common anode (+) and common cathode (-)

Each LED bar is either a common anode (+) or a common cathode (-). If it's a common anode (+), we connect the anode to **5V**, each other pin to a resistor, and the resistors to individual digital pins on the Arduino. For the common cathode (-), connect the cathode to the GND and each pin, using a resistor, to individual Arduino digital pins.

Bar graph variations

LED bar graphs come in multiple sizes and shapes. They can have 5 to 50 LEDs. There are some which are round. A lot of them have four to five colors of LEDs in one bar. Choose what fits your design or taste best.

See also

For other topics regarding LED assemblies, please check the following recipe:

▸ *The 7-segment display* recipe

The 7-segment display

Since the beginning of electronics, 7-segment displays have been used to display numbers. They are easy to connect and understand, and quite fun to use once they are properly implemented. We can use such a display to show the status of our system or to show data from a sensor.

Getting ready

The following ingredients are needed for this recipe:

▸ An Arduino board connected to the computer via USB

▸ A breadboard and jumper wires

▸ A 7-segment display

▸ Resistors between 220–1,000 ohm

How to do it...

Follow these steps in order to connect a 7-segment display to the Arduino:

1. Mount the 7-segment display on the breadboard.

2. If the display is a common anode (+) configuration, connect the common anode (+) pin to the **VCC** port on the Arduino. If it is a common cathode (-), connect the cathode to the **GND** port on the Arduino.

3. Connect each individual segment pin to one individual Arduino digital pin using a resistor.

Schematic

Here is one possible implementation of a common anode (+) 7-segment display:

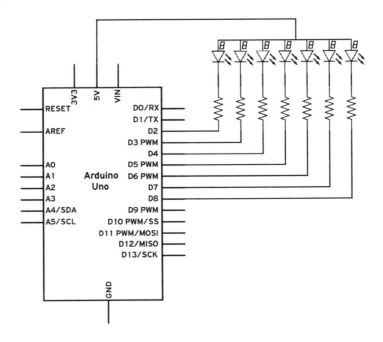

Here is one possible way of wiring it on a breadboard:

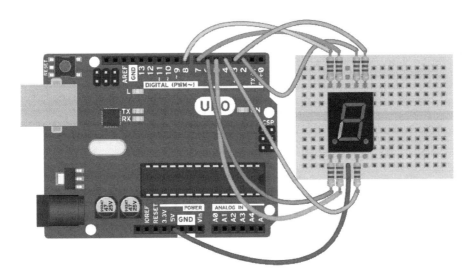

Code

The following code will make the 7-segment display countdown from 3 and restart:

```
// Declare the pins for the Segment display
int pinUP = 2;   // Upper segment
int pinUPR = 3;  // Up-right segment
int pinDWR = 4;  // Down-right segment
int pinDW = 5;   // Down segment
int pinDWL = 6;  // Down-left segment
int pinUPL = 7;  // Up-left segment
int pinCT = 8;   // Center segment

void setup() {
  // Declare the pins as Outputs
  pinMode(pinUP, OUTPUT);
  pinMode(pinUPR, OUTPUT);
  pinMode(pinDWR, OUTPUT);
  pinMode(pinDW, OUTPUT);
  pinMode(pinDWL, OUTPUT);
  pinMode(pinUPL, OUTPUT);
  pinMode(pinCT, OUTPUT);
}

void writeNumber(int value){
  // First we erase the previous value
  digitalWrite(pinUP, HIGH);
  digitalWrite(pinUPR, HIGH);
  digitalWrite(pinDWR, HIGH);
  digitalWrite(pinDW, HIGH);
  digitalWrite(pinDWL, HIGH);
  digitalWrite(pinUPL, HIGH);
  digitalWrite(pinCT, HIGH);
  // If we want to write 0
  if (value == 0){
    digitalWrite(pinUP, LOW);
    digitalWrite(pinUPR, LOW);
    digitalWrite(pinDWR, LOW);
    digitalWrite(pinDW, LOW);
    digitalWrite(pinDWL, LOW);
    digitalWrite(pinUPL, LOW);
  }

  // If we want to write 1
```

```
    if (value == 1){
      digitalWrite(pinUPR, LOW);
      digitalWrite(pinDWR, LOW);
    }

    // If we want to write 2
    if (value == 2){
      digitalWrite(pinUP, LOW);
      digitalWrite(pinUPR, LOW);
      digitalWrite(pinCT, LOW);
      digitalWrite(pinDWL, LOW);
      digitalWrite(pinDW, LOW);
    }
    // If we want to write 3
    if (value == 3){
      digitalWrite(pinUP, LOW);
      digitalWrite(pinUPR, LOW);
      digitalWrite(pinCT, LOW);
      digitalWrite(pinDWR, LOW);
      digitalWrite(pinDW, LOW);
    }
}


void loop(){
  // A resetting count-down
  writeNumber(3);
  delay(1000);

  writeNumber(2);
  delay(1000);

  writeNumber(1);
  delay(1000);

  writeNumber(0);
  delay(1000);
}
```

 This was designed for a common anode (+) configuration. For a common cathode (-) configuration, we need to change the digitalWrite functions to output the inverse. If it is HIGH it should output LOW, for example.

How it works...

A 7-segment display is made up of seven LEDs connected together in a certain physical pattern. If we control the seven segments individually, we can write any digit on the display and some letters too. Let's look into the code.

Code breakdown

The code makes the 7-segment display countdown from 3 to 0 and then reset. Here, we declare the individual pins for each LED segment on the display:

```
int pinUP = 2;   // Upper segment
int pinUPR = 3;  // Up-right segment
int pinDWR = 4;  // Down-right segment
int pinDW = 5;   // Down segment
int pinDWL = 6;  // Down-left segment
int pinUPL = 7;  // Up-left segment
int pinCT = 8;   // Center segment
```

In the `setup()` function, we set each LED pin as an output:

```
void setup() {
  pinMode(pinUP, OUTPUT);
  pinMode(pinUPR, OUTPUT);
  pinMode(pinDWR, OUTPUT);
  pinMode(pinDW, OUTPUT);
  pinMode(pinDWL, OUTPUT);
  pinMode(pinUPL, OUTPUT);
  pinMode(pinCT, OUTPUT);
}
```

The custom `writeNumber()` function takes a number we want to show on the display as the argument. After that, it erases the display and lights up each individual segment, in order to obtain the wanted pattern:

```
void writeNumber(int value){
  // First we erase the previous value
  digitalWrite(pinUP, HIGH);
  digitalWrite(pinUPR, HIGH);
  digitalWrite(pinDWR, HIGH);
  digitalWrite(pinDW, HIGH);
  digitalWrite(pinDWL, HIGH);
  digitalWrite(pinUPL, HIGH);
  digitalWrite(pinCT, HIGH);
  // If we want to write 1
```

```
    if (value == 1){
      digitalWrite(pinUPR, LOW);
      digitalWrite(pinDWR, LOW);
    }
  }
}
```

In the `loop()` function, we use our custom function to make the display count down:

```
void loop(){
  writeNumber(2);
  delay(1000);

  writeNumber(1);
  delay(1000);

  writeNumber(0);
  delay(1000);
}
```

There's more...

The 7-segment displays can be used in multiple applications. Displaying a digit value is the most used, however. In total, we can display all digits from 0 to 9, together with the letters A,b,c,C,d,E,F,h,and H. Here are a few things to consider:

Common anode (+) and common cathode (-)

Each 7-segment display is either common anode (+) or common cathode (-). If it's a common anode (+), we connect the anode to **5V** and each other pin with resistors to individual digital pins on the Arduino. For the common cathode (-), connect the cathode to the **GND** port and the other pins, using resistors, to individual Arduino digital pins.

The dot

Most 7-segment displays actually have an eighth segment. It's the small dot in the bottom right corner. When we use multiple 7-segments displays, we can use that dot to correctly represent, for example, the number 3.14.

Variations

The 7-segment display is just the most popular configuration. There are other types, such as the 9-segment, the 14-segment, and the 16-segment. On the 16-segment, any English character can be displayed.

3

Working with Buttons

In this chapter, we will cover the following recipes:

- ▶ Connecting a button
- ▶ Button with no resistor
- ▶ The toggle. switch
- ▶ Button to serial
- ▶ Button debouncing
- ▶ 1,000 buttons, 1 pin
- ▶ Button multiplexing

Introduction

Buttons are the basis of human interaction with the Arduino. We press a button, and something happens. They are simple components, as they only have two states: opened or closed. When a button is closed, current can pass though it. When it's opened, no current can pass. Some buttons are closed when we push them, some when they are released.

In this chapter, we will explore various button configurations and see how to tackle common problems with these. Let's jump in!

Connecting a button

One of the basic interactions you can have with the Arduino is pushing a button, which causes another action. Here, we will see how to connect and use a button.

To keep the example simple, we will connect a button to the Arduino, and whenever we press and hold it, the internal Arduino LED will light up. But first, we need to talk a little about buttons. There are a few common configurations found in everyday electronics. We can categorize buttons/switches based on three main characteristics:

▸ Momentary and maintained buttons

▸ Open or closed buttons

▸ Poles and throws

Momentary buttons are active as long as they are pressed, while **maintained** buttons keep the state we let them in. Keyboards have momentary buttons while the typical light switch is a maintained button.

Momentary buttons can either be opened or closed. This reflects the connection state when not pressed. A closed momentary switch will conduct current while not pressed and interrupt the current when pressed. An opened button will do the opposite.

Lastly, there are poles and throws. The following figure explains the main two types:

Single Pole Single Throw (**SPST**) switches have a closed state in which they conduct current, and an opened state in which they do not conduct current. Most momentary buttons are SPST.

Single Pole Double Throw (**SPDT**) switches route the current from the common pin to one of the two outputs. They are typically maintained; one example of this is the common light switch.

The common button we'll be using in this chapter is a push button. It's a small momentary opened switch. It typically comes in a 4-pin case:

The pins inside the two red ellipses are shorted together. When we press the button, all four pins are connected.

Getting ready

These are the ingredients needed to execute this recipe:

- An Arduino board connected to a computer via USB
- A breadboard and jumper wires
- A push button, which can be found at any electronics store, such as the online shops of Sparkfun, Radioshack, Adafruit, and Pololu
- A resistor between 1K–100K ohm

How to do it...

The following are the steps to connect a button:

1. Connect the Arduino **GND** and **5V** to separate long strips on the breadboard.
2. Mount the push button on the breadboard and connect one terminal to the **5V** long strip and the other to a digital pin on the Arduino—in this example, pin **2**.
3. Mount the resistor between the chosen digital pin and the **GND** strip. This is called a pull-down setup. More on this later.

Schematic

This is one possible implementation on the second digital pin. Other digital pins can also be used.

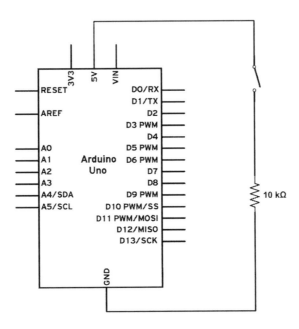

Here is an example of wiring it on a breadboard:

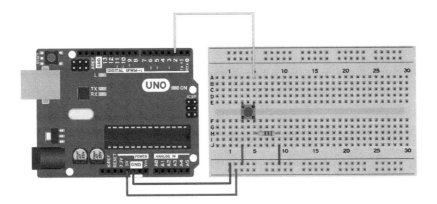

Code

The following code will read if the button has been pressed and will control the built-in LED:

```
// Declare the pins for the Button and the LED
int buttonPin = 2;
int LED = 13;

void setup() {
  // Define pin #2 as input
  pinMode(buttonPin, INPUT);
  // Define pin #13 as output, for the LED
  pinMode(LED, OUTPUT);
}

void loop() {
  // Read the value of the input. It can either be 1 or 0.
  int buttonValue = digitalRead(buttonPin);

  if (buttonValue == HIGH) {
    // If button pushed, turn LED on
    digitalWrite(LED,HIGH);
  } else {
    // Otherwise, turn the LED off
    digitalWrite(LED, LOW);
  }
}
```

 If the button is connected to a different pin, simply change the `buttonPin` value to the value of the pin that has been used.

How it works...

The purpose of the button is to drive the digital pin to which it's connected to either HIGH or LOW. In theory, this should be very simple: just connect one end of the button to the pin and the other to 5V. When not pressed, the voltage will be LOW; otherwise it will be 5V, HIGH. However, there is a problem. When the button is not pressed, the input will not be LOW but instead a different state called floating. In this state, the pin can be either LOW or HIGH depending on interference with other components, pins, and even atmospheric conditions!

That's where the resistor comes in. It is called a pull-down resistor as it pulls the voltage down to GND when the button is not pressed. This is a very safe method when the resistor value is high enough. Any value over 1K will work just fine, but 10K ohm is recommended.

Code breakdown

The code takes the value from the button. If the button is pressed, it will start the built-in LED. Otherwise, it will turn it off.

Here, we declare the pin to which the button is connected as pin 2, and the built-in LED on pin 13:

```
int buttonPin = 2;
int LED = 13;
```

In the `setup()` function, we set the button pin as a digital input and the LED pin as an output:

```
void setup() {
  pinMode(buttonPin, INPUT);
  pinMode(LED, OUTPUT);
}
```

The important part comes in the `loop()` function. The first step is to declare a variable that will equal the value of the button state. This is obtained using the `digitalRead()` function:

```
int buttonValue = digitalRead(buttonPin);
```

Lastly, depending on the button state, we initiate another action. In this case, we just light up the LED or turn it off:

```
if (buttonValue == HIGH){
        digitalWrite(LED,HIGH);
  } else {
    // Otherwise, turn the LED off
    digitalWrite(LED, LOW);
  }
```

There's more...

In this example, we've seen how to connect the button with a pull-down resistor. However, this is not the only way. It can also be connected using a pull-up resistor.

Pull-up configuration

In a pull-up configuration, the resistor will pull up the voltage to 5V when the button is not pressed. To implement it, connect one terminal of the button to the digital pin and the other one to GND. Now, connect the resistor between the digital pin and 5V.

This configuration will return inverted values. When pressed, the button will give LOW, not HIGH, as it will draw the pin down to GND, 0 V. However, it brings no advantages over the pull-down configuration.

Multiple buttons

What if we want to implement multiple buttons? We only need to use one digital pin configured as input for each button we use. Also, each button needs its independent pull-down or pull-up resistor.

See also

For other topics regarding buttons, check the following important recipes in this chapter:

▸ The *Button with no resistor* recipe

▸ The *Button to serial* recipe

▸ The *Button debouncing* recipe

Button with no resistor

It is simple to connect a button to the Arduino. You need the button, some wires, and a resistor. But what if we no longer need the resistor and want to still be able to use the button with no false readings?

The resistor is mandatory for proper operation of a button, and everybody will insist on using it. However, there is a little secret embedded in each Arduino pin. Each pin already has a pull-up resistor that we can enable with just one small change in our code.

Getting ready

For this recipe, you will need just two components:

▸ An Arduino board connected to a computer via USB

▸ A push button

How to do it...

There is just one simple step in this recipe:

1. Connect the Arduino GND to a terminal on the button and connect the chosen digital pin to the other terminal.

Schematic

Here is one implementation on the 12th digital pin. Other digital pins can also be used.

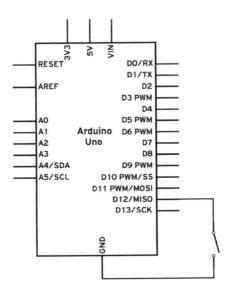

Here is a simple way of wiring the button:

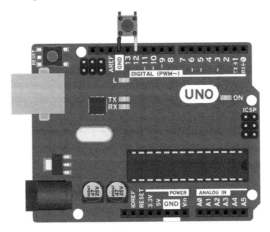

For most buttons with standard through-hole terminals, we can directly input the pins into the terminals on the Arduino.

Code

The following code will read if the button has been pressed and will control the built-in LED:

```
// Declare the pins for the Button and the LED
int buttonPin = 12;
int LED = 13;

void setup() {
  // Define pin #12 as input and activate the internal pull-up
resistor
  pinMode(buttonPin, INPUT_PULLUP);
  // Define pin #13 as output, for the LED
  pinMode(LED, OUTPUT);
}

void loop(){
  // Read the value of the input. It can either be 1 or 0
  int buttonValue = digitalRead(buttonPin);

  if (buttonValue == LOW){
    // If button pushed, turn LED on
    digitalWrite(LED,HIGH);
  } else {
    // Otherwise, turn the LED off
    digitalWrite(LED, LOW);
  }
}
```

 If the button is connected to a different pin, change the `buttonPin` value to the value of the pin that has been used.

How it works...

When we press the button, the value of the Arduino pin should be either LOW or HIGH. In this configuration, when we press the button, the pin is connected directly to GND, resulting in LOW. However, when it is not pressed, the pin will have no value; it will be in a floating state.

To avoid this, an internal pull-up resistor is connected between each pin and 5V. When we activate the resistor, it will keep the pin at HIGH until we press the button, thus connecting the pin to GND.

Code breakdown

The code takes the value from the button. If the button is pressed, it will start the built-in LED. Otherwise it will turn it off.

Here, we declare the pin to which the button is connected as pin 12, and the built-in LED as pin 13:

```
int buttonPin = 12;
int LED = 13;
```

In the `setup()` function, we set the button pin as a digital input and we activate the internal pull-up resistor using the `INPUT_PULLUP` macro. The LED pin is declared as an output:

```
void setup() {
  pinMode(buttonPin, INPUT_PULLUP);
  pinMode(LED, OUTPUT);
}
```

In the `loop()` function, we continuously read the value of the button using the `digitalRead()` function, and we store it in a newly declared variable called `buttonValue`:

```
int buttonValue = digitalRead(buttonPin);
```

Lastly, depending on the button state, we initiate another action. In this case, we just light up the LED or turn it off:

```
if (buttonValue == LOW) {
    // If button pushed, turn LED on
  digitalWrite(LED,HIGH);
} else {
  // Otherwise, turn the LED off
  digitalWrite(LED, LOW);
}
```

There's more...

It is easy to connect a button to the Arduino without any resistors. What if we need more buttons?

Multiple buttons

Each button requires its own digital pin and resistor. The Arduino already has one pull-up resistor in each digital and analog pin, so in the end, all that is needed is one pin for each individual button. The other terminal of the buttons is tied together to GND.

See also

For other topics regarding buttons, check the following important recipes in this chapter:

- The *Button to serial* recipe
- The *Button debouncing* recipe

The toggle switch

A toggle switch can be very useful for various projects. It can hold one or more constant states. For example, we can have a few of them and configure a certain system to work a certain way based on the configuration. This is done all the time on computer motherboards and other electronic devices.

A two-state toggle switch is just like a standard push button; only, it remains in the state we put it in. An on-off switch is a two-state toggle switch. It becomes more useful when we have a three-state toggle switch as in this recipe. It has two usable states and an off state.

In this recipe, we will use a basic toggle switch to light up two LEDs. When the toggle switch is in one end position, only one LED will be switched on. If it is in the other end position, the other LED will be switched on. Finally, if the toggle switch is in the center, both LEDs will be switched off.

Getting ready

The following are the ingredients required to execute this recipe:

- An Arduino board connected to a computer via USB
- A breadboard and jumper wires
- At least one toggle switch, which we can always take out of an old electric toy or buy from Sparkfun, Digikey, and so on
- Two LEDs and two resistors between 220–1,000 ohm

How to do it...

Follow these steps in order to connect the toggle switch to the LEDs:

1. Connect the Arduino GND to a long strip on the breadboard.
2. Mount the toggle switch and connect the middle terminal to the long GND strip on the breadboard.

3. Connect the other two terminals of the toggle switch to digital pins 2 and 3 on the Arduino board.

4. Mount the two LEDs and connect their ground terminal to the long GND strip on the breadboard.

5. Connect pin 5 to one of the LEDs using a resistor between pin 5 and the input of the LED. Do the same for pin 6 and the other LED.

Schematic

This is one possible implementation. Other digital pins can also be used.

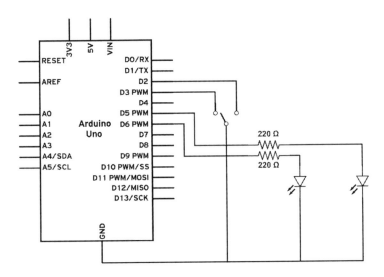

Here is a possible breadboard implementation:

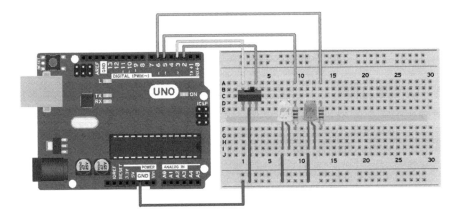

Code

The following code will check the status of the toggle switch and will drive the LEDs accordingly:

```
int buttonPin1 = 2;
int buttonPin2 = 3;

int LED1 = 5;
int LED2 = 6;

void setup() {
  // Define the two LED pins as outputs
  pinMode(LED1, OUTPUT);
  pinMode(LED2, OUTPUT);

  // Define the two buttons as inputs with the internal pull-up
resistor activated
  pinMode(buttonPin1, INPUT_PULLUP);
  pinMode(buttonPin2, INPUT_PULLUP);
}

void loop(){
  // Read the value of the inputs. It can be either 0 or 1
  // 0 if toggled in that direction and 1 otherwise
  int buttonValue1 = digitalRead(buttonPin1);
  int buttonValue2 = digitalRead(buttonPin2);


  if (buttonValue1 == HIGH && buttonValue2 == HIGH){
    // Switch toggled to the middle. Turn LEDs off
    digitalWrite(LED1, LOW);
    digitalWrite(LED2, LOW);

  } else if (buttonValue1 == LOW){
  // Button is toggled to the second pin
    digitalWrite(LED1, LOW);
    digitalWrite(LED2, HIGH);

  } else {
    // Button is toggled to the third pin
    digitalWrite(LED1, HIGH);
    digitalWrite(LED2, LOW);

  }

}
```

If the toggle switch is connected to other pins, simply change the `buttonPin1` and `buttonPin2` variables. The same goes for the LED pins.

How it works...

When the toggle switch is toggled to one of the two end positions, it will connect one of the Arduino pins to GND. The pin that is not connected to GND will stay HIGH due to the internal pull-up resistor in the Arduino pin. If the toggle switch is in the central position, no pin will be connected to GND and both will be HIGH.

Code breakdown

The code takes the value from the two pins connected to the toggle switch. If one of them goes LOW, it will turn on one of the LEDs.

Here, we declare the pins to which the toggle switch is connected as pins 2 and 3. The LEDs are defined on pins 5 and 6:

```
int buttonPin1 = 2;
int buttonPin2 = 3;

int LED1 = 5;
int LED2 = 6;
```

In the `setup()` function, we set the pins for the LEDs as outputs and the two pins going to the toggle switch as inputs. Also, we activate the internal pull-up resistor so that it does not need an external one:

```
void setup() {
  // Define the two LED pins as outputs
  pinMode(LED1, OUTPUT);
  pinMode(LED2, OUTPUT);

  // Define the two buttons as inputs with the internal pull-up
resistor activated
  pinMode(buttonPin1, INPUT_PULLUP);
  pinMode(buttonPin2, INPUT_PULLUP);
}
```

In the `loop()` function, we continuously read the values of the two pins going to the toggle switch, and we store them in the variables `buttonValue1` and `buttonValue2`:

```
int buttonValue1 = digitalRead(buttonPin1);
int buttonValue2 = digitalRead(buttonPin2);
```

Lastly, depending on the toggle switch state, we initiate another action:

```
if (buttonValue1 == HIGH && buttonValue2 == HIGH){
  // Switch toggled to the middle. Turn LEDs off
} else if (buttonValue1 == LOW){
// Button is toggled to the second pin, one LED ON
} else {
  // Button is toggled to the third pin, the other LED ON
}
```

There's more...

Toggle switches can be very useful when used together. A DIP switch is very interesting, as it usually has multiple small toggle switches. Each time we add a toggle switch, we double the number of configurations. With four two-state switches, we can have up to 16 configurations.

This is useful when we have a system that needs a lot of configurations. Rather than uploading code again and again, we can use the toggle switches to choose what to do.

See also

Use the following links to find some common switches you can buy:

- https://www.sparkfun.com/products/9276
- https://www.sparkfun.com/products/8034

Button to serial

If we want to easily track how a button acts, serial communication is the best and simplest way. All we need to do is to read the status of the button and print it to the serial connection.

Testing whether a button is working can be solved by using an LED. However, if we need to check two buttons or better understand what's happening when the button is pressed, serial communication is much safer and may even be simpler.

Getting ready

The following are the ingredients required to execute this recipe:

- An Arduino board connected to a computer via USB
- A button

How to do it...

This recipe uses the *Button with no resistor* recipe's hardware implementation. Please implement the same schematic as in that recipe. We will have different code here, which will output the values on the serial connection.

Code

The following code will print the button status on the serial connection:

```
int buttonPin = 2;

void setup() {
  // Define pin #2 as input
  pinMode(buttonPin, INPUT_PULLUP);

  // Establish the Serial connection with a baud rate of 9600
  Serial.begin(9600);
}

void loop(){
  // Read the value of the input. It can either be 1 or 0.
  int buttonValue = digitalRead(buttonPin);

  // Send the button value to the serial connection
  Serial.println(buttonValue);

  // Delays the execution to allow time for the serial transmission
  delay(25);
}
```

 If the button is connected to another digital pin, simply change the value of `buttonPin` to the digital pin that has been used.

How it works...

When the button is pressed, it can either return a value of 1 or 0. Because we activated the internal pull-up resistor inside the Arduino pin, the values will be safe, and no floating condition will be obtained. After we read the value of the pin, we send it to the serial connection.

Code breakdown

The code takes the value from the button connected to digital pin 2 and writes it to the serial.

In the `setup()` function, we set the button pin as an input and activate the internal pull-up resistor. Then, we start the Serial connection with a speed of 9,600 bits per second:

```
void setup() {
  pinMode(buttonPin, INPUT_PULLUP);
  Serial.begin(9600);
}
```

In the `loop()` function, we continuously read the value of the connected button:

```
int buttonValue = digitalRead(buttonPin);
```

Then, we print the value using the `Serial.println()` command. We can also use `Serial.print()`; however, `println` will write the value and go to a new line afterwards. This looks much better and it is easier to understand:

```
Serial.println(buttonValue);
```

At the end, we need a delay to allow the data to be transmitted. The delay can be short since we only send one value; however, it is mandatory to have it. Otherwise, the serial will constantly overflow and no good values will reach the computer:

```
delay(25);
```

There's more...

To print more than one button, we can use the `Serial.print()` function to write each button state in line and then use the `Serial.println()` function to go to the next line. Here is a simple implementation:

```
Serial.print(buttonValue1); // Print first value
Serial.print(" "); // Leave an empty space between
Serial.println(buttonValue2); // Print the second value
```

Button debouncing

A button is a simple device; when we push it, it gives a value, otherwise it gives another value. Unfortunately, it is not always like that. When we push or release a button, for a very small amount of time the button bounces between pushed or not. This is due to mechanical errors and wear and tear in the button.

Even if it is a small amount of time, the Arduino is quick, and when we press the button, it may read values that are quickly bouncing between pressed and not pressed. In most cases, this is not a problem; but in many cases, this happens and it can take hours to detect what is going wrong. Better be safe than sorry!

Another very important application of this is reading a button only once. When we press the button, we keep it pressed for a few milliseconds. In this time, the Arduino can read it hundreds, even thousands of times. It detects a few hundred times instead of once that we pushed the button. This is the primary use of debouncing in the Arduino world.

Getting ready

The following are the ingredients required for this recipe:

► An Arduino board connected to a computer via USB

► A button

How to do it...

This recipe uses the hardware implementation in the *Button with no resistor* recipe. Please implement the same schematic as in that recipe. We will have a different code here, which will output the debounced values on the serial connection.

Code

The following code will read the status of the button and print it over the serial connection:

```
// Declare the pin for the button
int buttonPin = 2;
// Variable for keeping the previous button state
int previousButtonValue = HIGH;

long lastDebounce = 0; // Last time the button was pressed
long debounceTime = 50; // Debounce delay

void setup() {
  // Define pin #2 as input and activate the internal pull-up
resistor
  pinMode(buttonPin, INPUT_PULLUP);
  // Establish the Serial connection with a baud rate of 115200
  Serial.begin(115200);
}

void loop(){
  // Read the value of the input. It can either be 1 or 0
  int buttonValue = digitalRead(buttonPin);
  if (buttonValue != previousButtonValue && millis() -
  lastDebounce >= debounceTime){
```

```
    // Reading is useable, print it
    Serial.println(buttonValue);

    // Reset the debouncing timer
    lastDebounce = millis();
    // Change to the latest button state
    previousButtonValue = buttonValue;
  }
  // Allow some delay for the Serial data to be transmitted
  delay(10);
}
```

> If the button is connected to another digital pin, change the value of `buttonPin` to the value of the digital pin that has been used.

How it works...

To avoid reading the button multiple times and detecting false readings, there are two important steps. First, we only read changes in the button state. If the button has the same value as at the last reading, we ignore it. Second—and here is the important step—if the button has been pressed or released, we don't evaluate its value for the following few milliseconds. This will make sure that no rapid oscillations in the button state are read.

It is possible to implement this with a simple `delay()` function; however, `delay()` stops the Arduino board from executing anything else.

Code breakdown

The code takes the value from the button connected on digital pin 2 and uses debouncing logic to assure proper output.

We need to declare a few variables. The `previousButtonValue` variable keeps track of the previous state of the button. The `lastDebounce` variable is important; it stores the particular time at which the button was pressed earlier. The `debounceTime` variable is the amount of time in milliseconds between each reading. It is important for these two variables to be declared as long type, because the numbers get pretty big quite fast.

```
int previousButtonValue = HIGH;

long lastDebounce = 0; // Last time the button was pressed
int debounceTime = 50; // Debounce delay
```

The Arduino keeps an internal count of time passed since the program began running. To access this time, we can use the `millis()` function, which returns the time in milliseconds.

In the `setup()` function, we set the button pin as an input and we activate the internal pull-up resistor. Then, we start the serial connection with a speed of 115,200 bits per second:

```
void setup() {
  pinMode(buttonPin, INPUT_PULLUP);
    Serial.begin(115200);
}
```

In the `loop()` function, we continuously read the value of the connected button:

```
int buttonValue = digitalRead(buttonPin);
```

Now we need to apply the debouncing part of the code. It consists of an `IF` clause with two conditions:

▸ The first condition checks whether the new reading is different from the last one. We don't want to detect a button push a hundred times when we press once.

▸ The second condition checks whether enough time has passed since the last reading. This makes sure the value doesn't bounce between states.

The time is declared in the `debounceTime` variable. A good value is around 50 milliseconds. It can be lower, but we will only need it to be lower if we want to press the button more than 20 times a second.

```
if (buttonValue != previousButtonValue && millis() - lastDebounce
>= debounceTime)
```

Then, we print the value using the `Serial.println()` command:

```
Serial.println(buttonValue);
```

It is very important on each usable reading to update the `lastDebounce` and `previousButtonValue` variables. These will be the new values that the debouncing filter will compare.

```
lastDebounce = millis();
previousButtonValue = buttonValue;
```

At the end, we need a short delay to allow the data to be transmitted:

```
delay(10);
```

See also

To clearly understand what contact bouncing is, visit http://en.wikipedia.org/wiki/Debounce#Contact_bounce.

1,000 buttons to 1 pin

One button, one pin—that is the way things are usually done on Arduino boards. But it is so limiting. There are some tricks that let you connect more than one button to a pin. Actually, it is even possible to connect 1,000 buttons to just 1 pin. We will explore this possibility in this recipe.

Getting ready

The following are the ingredients required for this recipe:

- An Arduino board connected to a computer via USB
- A breadboard and jumper wires
- Three buttons
- Four resistors of equal value: 1K ohm works well

How to do it...

We implement a simple configuration using only three buttons on the same pin. Here are the steps:

1. Connect the Arduino **GND** to a long strip on the breadboard. Also connect the Arduino **5V** to a long strip.
2. Connect one of the resistors from the **GND** strip to an analog pin—here, pin **A0**—on the Arduino.
3. Connect three resistors in series starting at the **5V** strip.
4. At each junction of two resistors, connect one button. Also connect the third button at the end of the resistor series.
5. Connect the other terminals of the buttons together and to the **A0** analog pin on the Arduino.

Schematic

This is one possible implementation. Other analog pins can also be used.

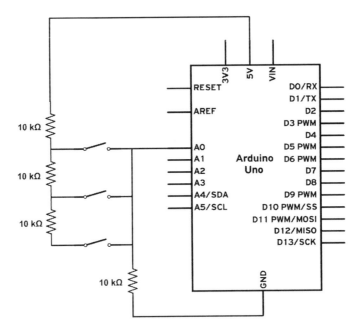

This is a possible breadboard implementation:

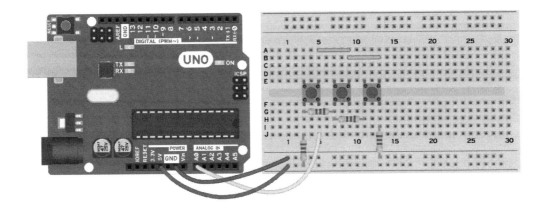

Code

The following code will read the analog pin on the Arduino board and detect which button is pressed:

```
// Declare the Analog pin on the Arduino board
int buttonPin = A0;

void setup() {

  // Establish the Serial connection with a baud rate of 9600
  Serial.begin(9600);
}

void loop(){
  // Read the value of the input. It can vary from 0 - 1023
  int buttonValue = analogRead(buttonPin);

  if (buttonValue < 200){
    // A value under 200 represents no button pushed
    Serial.println("0");
  } else if (buttonValue >= 200 && buttonValue < 300){
    // A value between 200 - 300 represents the third button
    Serial.println("S3");
  } else if (buttonValue >= 300 && buttonValue < 400){
    // A value between 300 - 400 represents the second button
    Serial.println("S2");
  } else if (buttonValue >= 400){
    // A value greater than 400 represents the first button
    Serial.println("S1");
  }


  // Delays the execution to allow time for the Serial transmission
  delay(25);
}
```

 If the buttons are connected to another analog pin, simply change the buttonPin variable to the analog pin that has been used.

How it works...

This is all possible due to an electric circuit called the voltage divider. Each time a button is pressed, a different voltage divider is created. Each button brings a different voltage to the analog pin on the Arduino. We can read this analog voltage and attribute a specific value to each button.

Code breakdown

The code takes the value from the analog pin and checks to which button it corresponds. It prints out on the serial which button has been pushed.

Here, we declare the analog pin that has been used:

```
int buttonPin = A0;
```

In the setup function, we start the serial connection with a speed of 9,600 bits per second:

```
void setup() {
   Serial.begin(9600);
}
```

In the `loop()` function, we continuously read the value of the analog pin, which can be from 0–1023:

```
int buttonValue = analogRead(buttonPin);
```

Then, we check which button is pressed. We should be able to attribute one exact value to each button. However, due to component tolerances and errors, it's much safer to use an interval. If the expected value is 250 and the button returns 251, the code will not detect the button. In this example, the intervals are extreme: 0–200 for no button, 200–300 for the third button, 300–400 for the second button, and over 400 for the first. The best way to find out the values is to make a simple program print the analog value of the pin on the serial:

```
if (buttonValue < 200){
    // A value under 200 represents no button pushed
    Serial.println("0");
  } else if (buttonValue >= 200 && buttonValue < 300){
    // A value between 200 - 300 represents the third button
    Serial.println("S3");
  } else if (buttonValue >= 300 && buttonValue < 400){
    // A value between 300 - 400 represents the second button
    Serial.println("S2");
  } else if (buttonValue >= 400){
    // A value greater than 400 represents the first button
    Serial.println("S1");
  }
```

In the end, always have some delay when working with serial communication to avoid overflow:

```
delay(25);
```

There's more...

This is a very useful solution when we need multiple buttons but have only a few pins left. Another advantage is the time needed to read the analog pin. It takes around 0.1 millisecond to read the analog pin, which solves some problems with debouncing.

Here are a few tips on how to easily do more with this configuration.

More buttons

The title says 1,000 but there are only three buttons here. However, the principle is the same. We can connect as many buttons as we have to a theoretical maximum of 1023. Each button needs a resistor, so for a configuration of 100 buttons, we will use 100 resistors in series and at each junction of two resistors, we will mount a button. Again, we will mount the hundredth button at the end. The Rd resistor that connects the pin to GND is also mandatory.

The values of the resistors are also very important. It is recommended to have a high value for the Rd resistor: somewhere between 100K–1M ohm. The other resistors should be equal to make things easier: somewhere between 1K–10K ohm.

Finding each button

The simplest way to find the value of every button connected is to print the value of the analog pin repeatedly while pressing the buttons one at a time. Each one should give a unique value and a value close to 0 when no button is pressed. Here is the code to print pin A0:

```
Serial.println(analogRead(A0));
delay(10);
```

Pressing multiple buttons

If we don't use too many buttons, we can actually detect multiple button presses. When we press two buttons, the resistors will be connected in parallel and the overall resistance will drop. This will cause the analog reading to be higher. Use the serial output to check what happens in your configuration.

See also

To understand how a voltage divider works, visit http://en.wikipedia.org/wiki/Voltage_divider.

Button multiplexing

Using a multiplexer, it is possible to make the Arduino read over a hundred buttons easily. A multiplexer/demultiplexer is an integrated circuit that selects one of several inputs and forwards them to the output. It requires a few control pins to determine which input to forward to the output.

Getting ready

Following are the ingredients required for this recipe:

- An Arduino board connected to a computer via USB
- A breadboard and jumper wires
- Four buttons
- A 4051 multiplexer or similar, which we can find at any electronics store and online at Digikey, Sparkfun, Adafruit, and so on

How to do it...

We implement a simple configuration using only four buttons. Here are the steps:

1. Connect the Arduino **GND** to a long strip on the breadboard. Also connect the Arduino **5V** to a long strip.

2. Mount the four buttons and connect one of their terminals to the long **GND** strip.

3. Connect the other terminal of each button to an individual input/output pin on the 4051—in this case, pins y0, y1, y2, and y3.

4. Connect the **E**, **VEE**, and **GND** pins of the 4051 multiplexer to the long **GND** strip.

5. Connect the **Vcc** pin on the 4051 to the **5V** strip on the breadboard.

6. Connect S0, S1, and S2 to three digital pins on the Arduino—in this example, 8, 9, and 10.

Schematic

This is one possible implementation. Other pins can also be used.

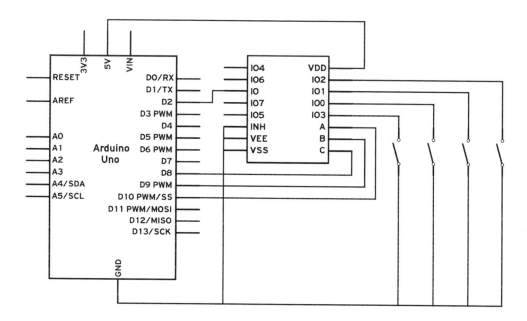

This is a possible breadboard implementation:

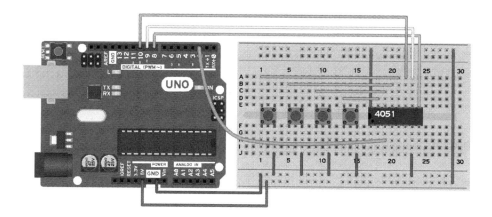

Code

The following code will read the four buttons connected to the multiplexer by switching the active pin on it:

```
// Define the input pin on the Arduino and the 3 selection pins
connected to the 4051
int buttonPin = 2;
int A = 10;
int B = 9;
int C = 8;

void setup() {
  // Define pin #2 as input with the pull up resistor on
  pinMode(buttonPin, INPUT_PULLUP);

  // Define the output pins going to the control lines of the
Multiplexer
  pinMode(A, OUTPUT);
  pinMode(B, OUTPUT);
  pinMode(C, OUTPUT);
  // Establish the Serial connection with a baud rate of 9600
  Serial.begin(9600);
}

void loop(){
  // We first read port IO0
  digitalWrite(A, LOW);
  digitalWrite(B, LOW);
  digitalWrite(C, LOW);
  int buttonIO0 = digitalRead(buttonPin);

  // Then we read port IO1
  digitalWrite(A, HIGH);
  digitalWrite(B, LOW);
  digitalWrite(C, LOW);
  int buttonIO1 = digitalRead(buttonPin);

  // Then we read port IO2
  digitalWrite(A, LOW);
  digitalWrite(B, HIGH);
  digitalWrite(C, LOW);
  int buttonIO2 = digitalRead(buttonPin);

  // Then we read port IO3
```

```
digitalWrite(A, HIGH);
digitalWrite(B, HIGH);
digitalWrite(C, LOW);
int buttonIO3 = digitalRead(buttonPin);

// Then we print to Serial the values
// We print them in-line separated by a space
Serial.print(buttonIO0);
Serial.print(" ");
Serial.print(buttonIO1);
Serial.print(" ");
Serial.print(buttonIO2);
Serial.print(" ");
Serial.println(buttonIO3);

// Delays the execution to allow time for the serial
delay(25);
}
```

How it works...

The multiplexer/demultiplexer is a useful component, but, a little tricky to understand.

Here we used a demultiplexer configuration. Each demultiplexer has one output and a number of inputs—in our case, eight. Also, it has control lines—in our example, three. Each control line represents a number: power of 2 minus 1. For the 4051, A = 1, B = 2 and C = 4. If we want to read input IO5, we set A and C to HIGH and S1 to LOW. This means the output will be connected to A + C = 5 input; therefore, pin IO5.

Basically, a multiplexer gives the power to connect one Arduino pin to one I/O pin on the multiplexer. Only one pin can be connected at any particular time.

Code breakdown

The code commands the connection on the multiplexer using the three command lines. It uses one input digital pin to get the value from the buttons and prints it on the serial connection.

Here, we declare the used pins:

```
int buttonPin = 2;
int A = 10;
int B = 9;
int C = 8;
```

In the `loop()` function, we set the multiplexer to each pin we want to read and we read it. In order to read pin IO0, we set A, B, and C to low, so their sum is 0. When we want to read pin 1, we set A to 1. IO3 will result A and B to HIGH:

```
digitalWrite(A, HIGH);
digitalWrite(B, LOW);
digitalWrite(C, LOW);
int buttonIO1 = digitalRead(buttonPin);
```

We do this for each button we want to read and then we print the output values on the serial.

There's more...

Here we have only four buttons on four pins—not a very good ratio of pins to buttons. However, for the same number of pins we can get eight buttons, as there are four free pins on the multiplexer.

More buttons

Even eight buttons on four pins is not too much. There are 16-channel multiplexers, such as the 4067 that require four control lines, totaling sixteen buttons on five pins. We can go even further! We can use more multiplexers, and we only need one new line for each multiplexer to connect to its output while sharing the control lines. Using a 4067 and all the pins, except 0 and 1, on the Arduino Uno, we can read 224 buttons. On the Arduino Mega, this will result in 800 buttons. The sky is the limit with multiplexers.

See also

For an in-depth explanation on multiplexers, visit `http://en.wikipedia.org/wiki/Multiplexer`.

4
Sensors

In this chapter, we will cover the following topics:

- Simple sensor – potentiometer
- Temperature sensor
- Detecting motion – PIR Sensor
- Measuring distance – infrared and ultrasonic
- Noise reduction
- Accelerometer
- Localization – GPS

Introduction

Acquiring data from the environment is the fundamental function of any autonomous system. And on the Arduino, this feature is so simple and powerful. We can find sensors for anything these days, from high radiation to sound. Most of them even share the same interface, so connecting and using them is easy once we understand the simple logic underneath. In this chapter, we will dive into the most common groups of sensors and we will see how easy it is to use them.

We can acquire interesting and useful sensors from DIY electronics and robotics shops. Online, These could be Sparkfun, Pololu, Adafruit, and Technobots, just to name a few.

Simple sensor – potentiometer

A **potentiometer**, also called a variable resistor, is a basic component that allows us to modify its internal resistance. We can use it to adjust settings in our program at any time. Or, we can use them to control things, such as a robotic hand or the intensity of a particular light. Here, we will make the built-in LED blink with a frequency that we will control via the potentiometer. We will also print the values over serial.

Getting ready

Following are the ingredients required for this recipe:

- An Arduino board connected to a computer via USB
- Jumper wires
- A 10K – 1M ohm potentiometer/variable resistor

How to do it...

Hooking up a potentiometer is easy, and here are the steps:

1. The potentiometer has three terminals. Connect the terminal in the center to an analog pin; here, we will connect it to **A2**.
2. Connect one of the other terminals to **GND**.
3. Connect the third terminal to **5V**.

Schematic

This is one possible implementation using pin **A2** as the analog input:

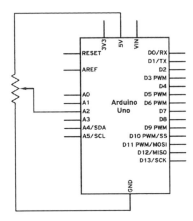

Here is an example of how to wire it:

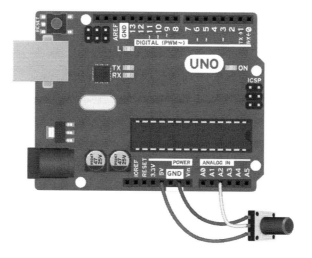

Code

The following code will read the value of the potentiometer, print it on the serial connection, and vary the LED pulsing frequency accordingly:

```
int LED = 13;        // Declare the built-in LED
int sensorPin = A2;  // Declare the analog port we connected

void setup(){
  // Start the Serial connection
  Serial.begin(9600);
  // Set the built in LED pin as OUTPUT
  pinMode(LED, OUTPUT);
}


void loop(){
  // Read the value of the sensor
  int val = analogRead(sensorPin);
  // Print it to the Serial
  Serial.println(val);

  // Blink the LED with a delay of a forth of the sensor value
  digitalWrite(LED, HIGH);
  delay(val/4);
  digitalWrite(LED, LOW);
  delay(val/4);
}
```

If the sensor is connected to another analog input, just change the `sensorPin` value to match the value of the input.

Rotate the potentiometer head and observe how the LED changes its pulsing frequency.

How it works...

Inside each Arduino there is an **Analog-to-Digital Converter** (**ADC**). This component can convert an analog signal value to a digital representation. ADCs come in a variety of ranges, accuracies, and resolutions. The integrated models from the Uno, Leonardo, and other normal Arduinos have a 10-bit resolution. This means that a voltage between 0 and 5 V on 5V Arduinos will be represented by a corresponding value between 0 and 1023. A voltage of 2.5 V will be equal to 512, which is half of the range.

We should never exceed the maximum voltage of the board on the analog inputs. In most boards, this is 5 V, but on the Due and a few others, the voltage can be 3.3 V. Let's see how the code works in the code breakdown.

A potentiometer works by adjusting the conductor length between the central and side terminals. It is recommended to use a high-resistance potentiometer; otherwise, a lot of current will pass through, heating it up. Any value over 10K ohm should be good.

Code breakdown

First, we declare two variables for the built-in LED and for the used analog port, to which we connected the potentiometer:

```
int LED = 13;
int sensorPin = A2;
```

In the `setup()` function, we start the serial connection and we declare the LED pin as an output:

```
void setup(){
  Serial.begin(9600);
  pinMode(LED, OUTPUT);
}
```

The deal breaker is the following function. It reads the analog value of the specified analog input and it returns it as a number between 0 and 1023. Remember that this conversion takes around 100 microseconds on most Arduino boards.

```
int val = analogRead(sensorPin);
```

And now we do two things. We print the value on the serial connection, and then we make the LED blink with an in-between delay of the read value divided by four, to make it blink fast:

```
Serial.println(val);
digitalWrite(LED, HIGH);
delay(val/4);
digitalWrite(LED, LOW);
delay(val/4);
```

There's more...

The `analogRead()` function is one of the most important functions on the Arduino platform. Almost every sensor uses this kind of interfacing. There are a few more things to know.

Arduino Due

The Arduino Due has a few great features on the analog side. First of all, it has an integrated 12-bit ADC, so it can return more precise values between 0 and 4095. However, it comes preconfigured to only output 10 bit. We can change that using the `analogReadResolution(bits)` function.

For example, `analogReadResolution(12)` will make the `analogRead()` function output 12-bit values.

 Remember that the Due is designed for a maximum of 3.3 V, not 5 V; applying more than 3.3 V will damage the board.

Analog reference (AREF)

Most Arduinos have an AREF pin that enables us to give the voltage range on which the ADC will return. So if we input 2 V to the AREF pin and configure the code, it will output 1023 for 2V and 0 for 0V. This feature is useful if we have sensors that output less than 5V and we need more precision.

To tell the Arduino we are using an external reference on AREF, we need to use the `analogReference(type)` function. The `type` argument can take the following values:

▸ DEFAULT: This is the standard configuration with a range from 0 V to 5 V

▸ EXTERNAL: This will use the value on AREF for reference

Another important thing to remember is to use the `analogReference()` function first, before using the `analogRead()` function. If the reference type is not set to EXTERNAL, but we do apply a voltage to AREF, when we use the `analogRead()` function we will basically short the microcontroller. This can damage the board.

For more details about other types of analog references, check the *See also* section.

See also

For more information on the Arduino Due `analogReadResolution()` function and more analog references, visit the following links:

▸ `http://arduino.cc/en/Reference/AnalogReadResolution`

▸ `http://arduino.cc/en/Reference/AnalogReference`

Temperature sensor

Almost all sensors use the same analog interface. Here, we explore a very useful and fun sensor that uses the same. Temperature sensors are useful for obtaining data from the environment. They come in a variety of shapes, sizes, and specifications. We can mount one at the end of a robotic hand and measure the temperature in dangerous liquids. Or we can just build a thermometer.

Here, we will build a small thermometer using the classic LM35 and a bunch of LEDs.

Getting ready

The following are the ingredients required for this recipe:

▸ An Arduino board connected to a computer via USB

▸ A LM35 temperature sensor

▸ A breadboard and jumper wires

▸ A bunch of LEDs, different colors for a better effect

▸ Some resistors between 220–1,000 ohm

How to do it...

The following are the steps to connect a button without a resistor:

1. Connect the LEDs next to each other on the breadboard.

2. Connect all LED negative terminals—the cathodes—together and then connect them to the Arduino **GND**.

3. Connect a resistor to each positive terminal of the LED. Then, connect each of the remaining resistor terminals to a digital pin on the Arduino. Here, we used pins 2 to 6.

4. Plug the LM35 in the breadboard and connect its ground to the **GND** line. The **GND** pin is the one on the right, when looking at the flat face.

5. Connect the leftmost pin on the LM35 to **5V** on the Arduino.

6. Lastly, use a jumper wire to connect the center LM35 pin to an analog input on the Arduino. Here we used the **A0** analog pin.

Schematic

This is one possible implementation using the pin **A0** for analog input and pins 2 to 6 for the LEDs:

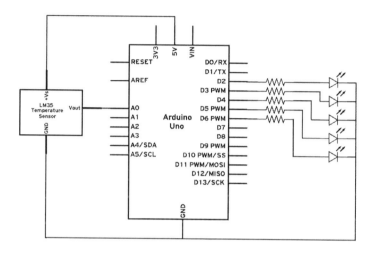

Here is a possible breadboard implementation:

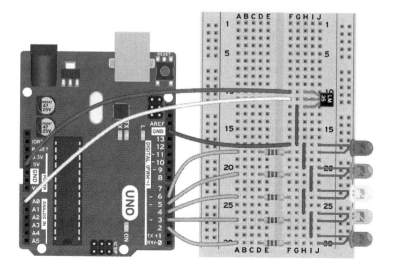

Code

The following code will read the temperature from the LM35 sensor, write it on the serial, and light up the LEDs to create a thermometer effect:

```
// Declare the LEDs in an array
int LED [5] = {2, 3, 4, 5, 6};
int sensorPin = A0; // Declare the used sensor pin

void setup(){
  // Start the Serial connection
  Serial.begin(9600);
  // Set all LEDs as OUTPUTS
  for (int i = 0; i < 5; i++){
    pinMode(LED[i], OUTPUT);
  }
}

void loop(){
  // Read the value of the sensor
  int val = analogRead(sensorPin);
  Serial.println(val); // Print it to the Serial

  // On the LM35 each degree Celsius equals 10 mV
  // 20C is represented by 200 mV which means 0.2 V / 5 V * 1023 = 41
  // Each degree is represented by an analogue value change of
  approximately 2

  // Set all LEDs off
  for (int i = 0; i < 5; i++){
    digitalWrite(LED[i], LOW);
  }

if (val > 40 && val < 45){ // 20 - 22 C
    digitalWrite( LED[0], HIGH);
  } else if (val > 45 && val < 49){ // 22 - 24 C
    digitalWrite( LED[0], HIGH);
    digitalWrite( LED[1], HIGH);
  } else if (val > 49 && val < 53){ // 24 - 26 C
    digitalWrite( LED[0], HIGH);
    digitalWrite( LED[1], HIGH);
    digitalWrite( LED[2], HIGH);
  } else if (val > 53 && val < 57){ // 26 - 28 C
    digitalWrite( LED[0], HIGH);
```

```
      digitalWrite( LED[1], HIGH);
      digitalWrite( LED[2], HIGH);
      digitalWrite( LED[3], HIGH);
    } else if (val > 57){ // Over 28 C
      digitalWrite( LED[0], HIGH);
      digitalWrite( LED[1], HIGH);
      digitalWrite( LED[2], HIGH);
      digitalWrite( LED[3], HIGH);
      digitalWrite( LED[4], HIGH);
    }
    delay(100); // Small delay for the Serial to send
}
```

Blow into the temperature sensor to observe how the temperature goes up or down.

How it works...

The LM35 is a very simple and reliable sensor. It outputs an analog voltage on the center pin that is proportional to the temperature. More exactly, it outputs 10 mV for each degree Celsius. For a common value of 25 degrees, it will output 250 mV, or 0.25 V. We use the ADC inside the Arduino to read that voltage and light up LEDs accordingly.

If it's hot, we light up more of them, if not, less. If the LEDs are in order, we will get a nice thermometer effect.

Code breakdown

First, we declare the used LED pins and the analog input to which we connected the sensor. We have five LEDs to declare so, rather than defining five variables, we can store all five pin numbers in an array with 5 elements:

```
int LED [5] = {2, 3, 4, 5, 6};
int sensorPin = A0;
```

We use the same array trick to simplify setting each pin as an output in the setup() function. Rather than using the pinMode() function five times, we have a for loop that will do it for us. It will iterate through each value in the LED[i] array and set each pin as output:

```
void setup(){
  Serial.begin(9600);
  for (int i = 0; i < 5; i++){
    pinMode(LED[i], OUTPUT);
  }
}
```

In the `loop()` function, we continuously read the value of the sensor using the `analogRead()` function; then we print it on the serial:

```
int val = analogRead(sensorPin);
Serial.println(val);
```

At last, we create our thermometer effect. For each degree Celsius, the LM35 returns 10 mV more. We can convert this to our `analogRead()` value in this way: 5V returns 1023, so a value of 0.20 V, corresponding to 20 degrees Celsius, will return 0.20 V/5 V * 1023, which will be equal to around 41.

We have five different temperature areas; we'll use standard if and else casuals to determine which region we are in. Then we light the required LEDs.

There's more...

Almost all analog sensors use this method to return a value. They bring a proportional voltage to the value they read that we can read using the `analogRead()` function.

Here are just a few of the sensor types we can use with this interface:

Temperature	Humidity	Pressure	Altitude	Depth	Liquid level
Distance	Radiation	Interference	Current	Voltage	Inductance
Resistance	Capacitance	Acceleration	Orientation	Angular velocity	Magnetism
Compass	Infrared	Flexing	Weight	Force	Alcohol
Methane and other gases	Light	Sound	Pulse	Unique ID such as fingerprint	Ghost!

Detecting motion – PIR sensor

Ever wondered how those motion sensors work? Usually, we find them in lights that turn up when we move. Almost all of them use a simple and common sensor called a Passive Infrared (PIR) sensor.

Here, we will build one of those annoying movement-sensitive lights, using an Arduino, its built-in LED, and a PIR sensor.

Getting ready

The following are the ingredients needed to execute this recipe:

  ▸   An Arduino board connected to a computer via USB

- ▸ Jumper wires
- ▸ A PIR sensor

How to do it...

Hooking up a PIR sensor is easy:

1. It has three terminals. One is the voltage input, one is the ground, and the last one is the data pin.

2. Connect the ground on the PIR to one of the **GND** pins on the Arduino. Connect the voltage input to **5V**, and finally, connect the data pin to one digital pin. Here we used pin **2**.

Schematic

This is one possible implementation using pin **D2** as the input:

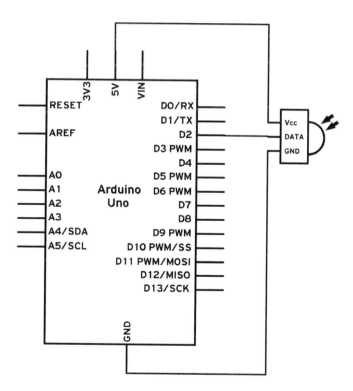

Here is an example of how to wire it:

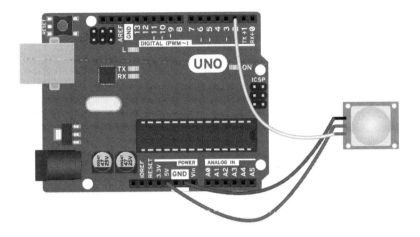

Code

The following code will read the value of the digital pin on which the PIR sensor is connected. If it detects motion, it will make the LED blink:

```
int LED = 13;        // Declare the built-in LED
int sensorPin = 2;   // Declare the used sensor pin

void setup(){
  // Set the LED pin as OUTPUT
  pinMode(LED, OUTPUT);
  // Set the sensor pin as digital input and activate the internal
  pull-up resistor
  pinMode(sensorPin, INPUT_PULLUP);

  // Wait for the sensor to take a snapshot of the room
  // Approximately 1-2 seconds
  delay(3000); // We are waiting 3
}

void loop(){
  // Read the sensor, if it goes low, we blind the LED for 1 second
  if (digitalRead(sensorPin) == LOW){
    digitalWrite(LED, HIGH);
    delay(1000);
```

```
        digitalWrite(LED, LOW);
    }
}
```

How it works...

The PIR sensor uses the radiated temperature of every object it sees in the infrared spectrum. The first time it powers up, it records how the area in front looks and then it compares everything to that. If it sees a significant difference, such as a human passing by, it will pull its data pin to LOW, thus alerting us to the movement.

Code breakdown

Firstly, we declare the digital pin and the built-in LED we have used:

```
int LED = 13;
int sensorPin = 2;
```

The PIR initially takes a snapshot of the environment it is in. This process takes around one or two seconds so we can wait for around three seconds, in the `setup()` function, to make sure the sensor is up and ready. Also, we declare the pin we used as `INPUT_PULLUP`.

The sensor will pull down the voltage once it detects motion, but for that it needs some voltage to pull down. By configuring the input as a pullup, we activate the built-in resistor on the pin that will bring the voltage up to 5V:

```
void setup(){
  pinMode(LED, OUTPUT);
  pinMode(sensorPin, INPUT_PULLUP);
  delay(3000);
}
```

In the `loop()` function, we continuously check whether the sensor detects motion by pulling down the voltage. This will return the LOW voltage for which we are looking. Once we detect motion, we simply get the LED to blink, to make a less annoying motion-activated light:

```
    if (digitalRead(sensorPin) == LOW){
      digitalWrite(LED, HIGH);
      delay(1000);
      digitalWrite(LED, LOW);
    }
```

Measuring distance – infrared and ultrasonic

A distance sensor is the most important sensor for any robot. It's usually referred to as the "eyes" of a robot. Distance sensors are very useful as we can make systems that react based on how close we are to them or based on the presence of various obstacles.

There are two common technologies used in amateur distance sensing: infrared sensors, such as the classic Sharp IR, and ultrasonic sensors, usually called **sonars**. Now, let's build a distance-controlled LED!

Getting ready

To build a distance-controlled LED, we will need the following ingredients:

- An Arduino board connected to a computer via USB
- One LED
- A Sharp infrared proximity sensor such as the GP2Y0A21YK or the GP2Y0A02YK0F

How to do it...

Connecting a Sharp IR is easy. Maybe this is why it's so popular. Follow these simple steps to connect one:

1. Each Sharp IR has three pins. One is the power input, which we connect to **5V**. Another is the ground that we will connect to one **GND** pin. Lastly, there is the analog output pin that needs to be connected to an analog input. Here, we used pin **A0**.

2. We will make a small illegal connection here. We will directly connect the LED to the Arduino without any resistor. For low-power LEDs, there is no problem, and neither the Arduino nor the LED will be affected. Plug the negative terminal to **GND** and the other terminal to one of the pins close by. Here, we used pin **11** for its PWM functionality.

 But please don't exceed a 3 mm, 10–20 mA LED. No high-power LEDs here! It could easily fry the LED or the Arduino. If we don't know how powerful our LED is, we should just mount a 220-ohm resistor in series.

Schematic

This is one possible implementation using pin **A0** as the analog input and pin **11** as the LED output:

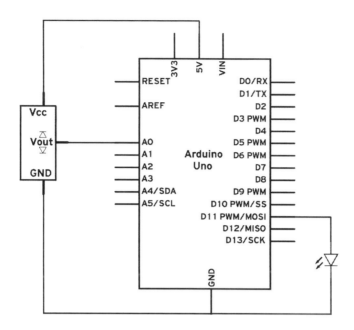

Here is an example of how to wire it:

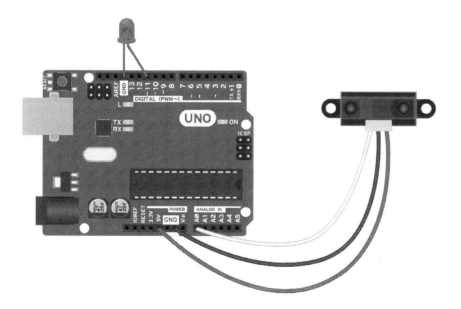

Code

The following code will read the value of the sensor, print it on the serial connection, and vary the LED intensity using PWM, to match the distance:

```
int sensorPin = A0; // Declare the used sensor pin
int LED = 11; // Declare the connected LED

void setup(){
  Serial.begin(9600); // Start the Serial connection
}

void loop(){
  // Read the analog value of the sensor
  int val = analogRead(A0);
  // Print the value over Serial
  Serial.println(val);
  // Write the value to the LED using PWM
  analogWrite(LED, val/4);
  // Wait a little for the data to print
  delay(100);
}
```

How it works...

Sharp IR sensors measure distance using an infrared beam that reflects on the object before it. The infrared beam is projected at a small angle. When it hits an object, it is reflected at a different angle, depending on the distance to the object. The sensor detects this angle and outputs the distance.

Code breakdown

First, we declare two variables for the built-in LED and for the used analog port to which we connected the Sharp IR sensor:

```
int sensorPin = A0;
int LED = 11;
```

In the `setup()` function, we only start the serial connection. We don't need to declare the LED pin as output because we use the `analogWrite()` function, which doesn't require a declaration.

In the `loop()` function, we read the sensor, write the value over serial, and then set the intensity of the LED using PWM. Since PWM takes values from 0 to 255 and the `analogRead()` function returns values from 0 to 1023, we divide the value of `analogRead()` by 4 when we use it in `analogWrite()`.

There's more...

Distance sensors have a huge market with hundreds upon hundreds of different models. Generally, in the cheap, hobbyist section, we can either find infrared sensors—such as the Sharp IR—or ultrasonic sensors.

An infrared sensor has a very narrow sensing beam. This means it can detect objects in tight places without interfering with other objects. However, if an object is too thin or has holes in its body, the sensor beam might go through it and give false readings.

An ultrasonic sensor, typically called sonar, uses sound above the normal hearing frequency to detect distance. It does so by emitting a short sound pulse and waiting for it to return. It measures the time it takes for the sound to travel, bounce on objects, and then travel back to the sensor.

Because the speed of sound is known, the total time it takes for the sound to return is dependent on the distance to the objects. This creates a very wide sensing beam. It is useful in many applications, especially when we need to detect large, complex objects. However, the wide beam will create interference if we have two objects in range. It will always detect the closer one.

An important thing to remember is that infrared sensors are dependent on the color of the measured objects while sonar is generally not affected by parameters except the shape and distance of the object.

See also

Here are a few references about how sensors work:

- ▸ http://www.societyofrobots.com/sensors_sonar.shtml
- ▸ The *Noise reduction* recipe for the better handling of sensor data

Noise reduction

Noise is everywhere. This world is made of noise. This is what everybody related to sensors will constantly repeat. But what is noise? It's unexpected data generated by sensors or signal sources. It can completely ruin the behavior of an autonomous system if not treated properly.

Here, we will use the implementation from the *Measuring distance – infrared and ultrasonic* recipe. The Sharp IR is known for its interference with basically anything, and here we will explore two standard methods of filtering the data generated by the sensor.

Getting ready

The following are the ingredients needed for this recipe:

▸ An Arduino board connected to a computer via USB

▸ A Sharp infrared proximity sensor such as the GP2Y0A21YK or the GP2Y0A02YK0F

How to do it...

This recipe uses the implementation from the *Measuring distance – infrared and ultrasonic* recipe. Please implement the same circuit as you did there.

Code

The following code will read the output of the Sharp IR sensor and will use two filtering methods to filter it and then print it over the serial connection:

```
int sensorPin = A0; // Declare the used sensor pin

// Function that reads a sensor with specified number of samples
// Returns the mean filtered value
int readMean(int pin, int samples){
  // Variable to store the sum of readings
  int sum = 0;
  // Read the samples and add them all
  for (int i = 0; i < samples; i++){
    sum = sum + analogRead(pin);
  }
  // Divide the sum by the number of samples
  sum = sum/samples;
  // Return the sum
  return sum;
}


// Function that reads a sensor with specified number of samples
// Returns the median filtered value
int readMedian (int pin, int samples){
  // Variable to store the readings
  int raw[samples];
  // Read the samples each as a value in the vector
  for (int i = 0; i < samples; i++){
```

```
    raw[i] = analogRead(pin);
  }

  // Sort the values
  // Lazy bubble sort
  int temp = 0; // temp value
  for (int i = 0; i < samples; i++){
    for (int j = i; j < samples - 1; j++){
      // Check if values out of order
      if (raw[j] > raw[j + 1]){
        // If so, swap them
        temp = raw[j];
        raw[j] = raw[j + 1];
        raw[j + 1] = temp;
      }
    }
  }

  // Return the middle value
  return raw[samples/2];
}

void setup(){
  // Start the Serial connection
  Serial.begin(9600);
}

void loop(){
  // Print the normal value and then a space
  Serial.print(analogRead(sensorPin));
  Serial.print(" ");
  // Print the mean filtered value and then a space
  Serial.print(readMean(sensorPin, 15));
  Serial.print(" ");
  // Print the median filtered value
  Serial.println(readMedian(sensorPin, 15));
  // Short delay for the Serial
  delay(100);
}
```

How it works...

There are hundreds of noise reduction filters, each with their own advantages and disadvantages. Here, we explore two very common and useful ones: the mean filter and the median filter. A filter takes some values and uses the relation between them to figure out which one is closer to reality.

Noise for a Sharp IR, for example, can be a random reading of 80 cm when the object is at 25 cm. The sensor might continuously output 25 cm and then suddenly, just for one reading, output a glitch of 80 cm. This can cause catastrophic effects on any autonomous system that is critically dependent on the distance.

Let's look at each of the two algorithms individually.

Mean filter

The mean filter takes a few readings and then averages them. This generally reduces noise, but at the expense of a lower response rate. Because we have to read multiple samples and average them, we increase the required time and decrease the overall response frequency. Most of the time, this is not a luxury and it is required. Good and slow values are much better than bad values.

1. We declare a function with two parameters: one will be the pin to which the sensor is connected, and the second one will be the number of samples:

    ```
    int readMean(int pin, int samples){
    ```

2. Then we continuously read the analog input using a for loop while adding the values to a sum variable:

    ```
    int sum = 0;
    for (int i = 0; i < samples; i++){
        sum = sum + analogRead(pin);
      }
    ```

3. And here comes the averaging. We divide the sum of all samples by the number of samples, thus obtaining the average value:

    ```
    sum = sum/samples;
    ```

In the end, we just return this averaged sum value using `return sum`.

Median filter

The median filter is a bit more complicated but very powerful. It is much more responsive than the mean filter, as it doesn't manipulate the values in any way. It works on the assumption that noise will be both overshooting and undershooting. Overshooting means that the returned value is greater than the actual value while undershooting is the opposite.

The filter works by taking a number of samples, sorting them in ascending order, and then returning the central value. Usually, if the noise is roughly equal in both directions, the filtered value will be the expected value.

1. As with the mean filter, we declare a function with a pin and a sample parameter:

    ```
    int readMedian (int pin, int samples){
    ```

2. Then we declare an array to hold all the values that we also read in a for loop:

    ```
    int raw[samples];
    for (int i = 0; i < samples; i++){
        raw[i] = analogRead(pin);
    }
    ```

Here comes the important part—sorting the array. Here we use a bubble sort, the laziest of all sorting algorithms, but also the easiest to understand and implement. Take a look at the *See also* section for more information about it. The algorithm will return a sorted vector with the smallest samples at the beginning and the largest ones at the end of it.

Lastly, we return the value in the center, which should be very close to the expected value:

```
return raw[samples/2];
```

Main loop()

In the `loop()` function we just print the normal value, the mean filtered value, and the median filtered value, all using a serial connection:

```
Serial.print(analogRead(sensorPin));
Serial.print(" ");
Serial.print(readMean(sensorPin, 15));
Serial.print(" ");
Serial.println(readMedian(sensorPin, 15));
delay(100);
```

To test, set a sample size of 15 and run the code. Move an object in front of the sensor and then copy the data and put it in chart-generating software such as Microsoft Office Excel. Vary the sample size until it fits your application.

See also

For more about the bubble sort algorithm, visit `http://en.wikipedia.org/wiki/Bubble_sort`.

Accelerometer

Accelerometers are advanced components that can measure acceleration. Initially, they were designed for airplanes and rockets, but now we can find them in any phone, laptop, hard drive, and a whole bunch of toys.

By measuring acceleration, we can determine if an object is moving, how rapidly it is changing direction, and benefit from its most popular use—determining the orientation of the object. Accelerometers come in various types and the number of axes they can sense is the basis of their categorization. Now, almost all accelerometers can sense three axes—meaning they can sense acceleration in any direction it happens.

In this example, we will read the data from the accelerometer and print it over a serial connection.

Getting ready

To execute this recipe, you will need the following ingredients:

▶ An Arduino board connected to a computer via USB

▶ An analog accelerometer board; in this case, we used Sparkfun ADXL335

▶ A breadboard and jumper wires

How to do it...

Analog accelerometers are not difficult to connect. These steps should make it all work:

1. Identify the voltage supply on the accelerometer board. It's typically labeled with **VCC** or **5V**. Connect it to the Arduino **5V**. Also connect the accelerometer **GND** to the Arduino **GND**.

2. Each axis should have an analog output pin. Connect each analog output to an analog input on the Arduino. Here we used analog inputs **A0**, **A1**, and **A2** on the Arduino.

Schematic

The following is a possible implementation using an ADXL335 accelerometer breakout board from Sparkfun:

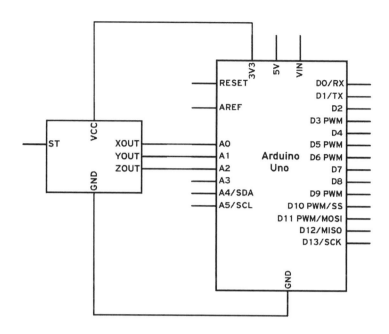

Here is an example of how to wire it:

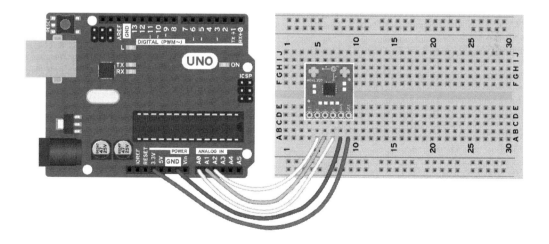

Code

The following code will read the values from the accelerometer and print them to the serial connection. If it detects movement, it will also blink the built-in LED:

```
// Declare built-in LED pin
int LED = 13;

// Declare the X,Y,Z analog pins
int xPin = A0;
int yPin = A1;
int zPin = A2;

void setup(){
    Serial.begin(9600);
  pinMode(LED, OUTPUT);
}

void loop(){
  // Read the 3 values
  int xVal = analogRead(xPin);
  int yVal = analogRead(yPin);
  int zVal = analogRead(zPin);

  // Print the 3 values on the Serial
  Serial.print(xVal);
  Serial.print(" ");
  Serial.print(yVal);
  Serial.print(" ");
  Serial.println(zVal);

  // Check for movement
  // Values at rest:
  // X ~ 330
  // Y ~ 330
  // Z ~ 400
  // If movement, blink the built-in LED
  if (xVal < 310 || xVal > 350 || yVal < 310 || yVal > 350 || zVal
  < 380 || zVal > 420){
    digitalWrite(LED, HIGH);
    delay(300);
```

```
    digitalWrite(LED, LOW);
  }

  // Small delay for the Serial
  delay(50);
}
```

How it works...

Accelerometers have different technologies to make them read acceleration. The most used one in embedded electronics is MEMS. Inside the sensor, we can find some parts that are freely moving. When this is happening, they change their internal resistance, and so output a different voltage based on the amount of movement. Take a look at the *See also* section for a more detailed explanation.

Code breakdown

After we declare the used pins in individual variables, we declare the LED pin as an output in the `setup()` function. There, we also initiate the serial connection.

In the `loop()` function, we first read the values of the three accelerometer outputs:

```
    int xVal = analogRead(xPin);
    int yVal = analogRead(yPin);
    int zVal = analogRead(zPin);
```

Then we print them over the serial, one next to the other. When the sensor is standing still on a flat surface, it returns values of around 330, 330, and 400 on the *x*, *y*, and *z* axes respectively. However, if we move or incline it, the values will rapidly change. The following long `if` clause checks for each analog pin, if movement was detected, by checking against an interval. If any of the pins exceed the specified interval, the Arduino will blink the internal LED:

```
  if (xVal < 310 || xVal > 350 || yVal < 310 || yVal > 350 || zVal <
    380 || zVal > 420){
      digitalWrite(LED, HIGH);
      delay(300);
      digitalWrite(LED, LOW);
  }
```

There's more...

Accelerometers are very handy for measuring movement and orientation. If we integrate the acceleration over time, we can find out how much an object moved. The problem is that they are very susceptible to vibrations, which can completely ruin the readings. In most mobile phones, an **Inertial Measurement Unit** (**IMU**), which combines an accelerometer and a gyroscope, is used to obtain better orientation readings.

See also

To understand how an accelerometer works, visit `http://www.explainthatstuff.com/accelerometers.html`.

Localization – GPS

The **Global Positioning System** (**GPS**) uses an array of satellites orbiting around the Earth and sending time information. A GPS receiver picks up the signal transmitted from the satellites, calculates the time it took for the signal to arrive, and by identifying the position of the satellites, triangulates the position on the surface of the globe.

GPS is very useful in autonomous cars, RC planes or drones, and data logging applications. Here, we will learn how to read the data from a GPS, which is surprisingly easy. In this recipe, we will use the `SoftwareSerial` library that is better detailed in the Communication chapter.

Getting ready

Following are the ingredients needed for this recipe:

- An Arduino board connected to a computer via USB
- Jumper wires and a breadboard
- A UART-compatible 5V GPS receiver such as the Copernicus

How to do it...

Hooking up a potentiometer is easy and here are the steps:

1. Plug the GPS receiver into the breadboard.
2. Connect the ground and power on the GPS to the **GND** and **5V** lines on the Arduino.
3. Connect the TX of the GPS to a digital pin on the Arduino. Here we used pin **8**.
4. Connect the RX of the GPS to another digital pin on the Arduino. Here we used pin **9**.

Schematic

This is one possible implementation using pins **8** and **9** for a soft serial:

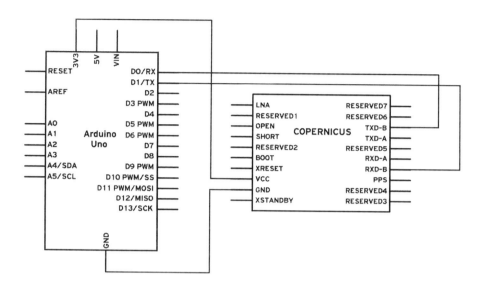

Here is an example of how to wire it:

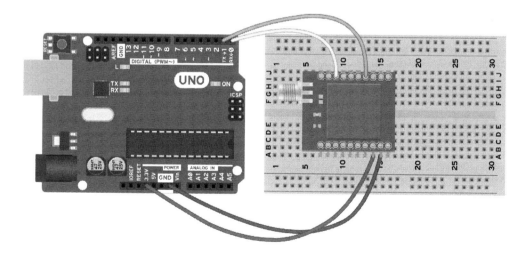

Code

The following code will read the output of the GPS using a soft serial connection and write it to the computer using the real serial port:

```
// Include the Software Serial library
#include <SoftwareSerial.h>

// Define a Software Serial object and the used pins
// Connect GPS TX to Soft Serial RX and GPS RX to Soft Serial TX
SoftwareSerial softSerial(8, 9); // RX, TX

void setup(){
  Serial.begin(9600); // Normal Serial
  softSerial.begin(9600); // Soft Serial
}

void loop(){
  // Check for received characters from the GPS
  if (softSerial.available()){
    // Write what is received to the real serial
    Serial.write(softSerial.read());
  }
}
```

How it works...

A GPS sensor constantly outputs a string full of information via a serial port. Generally, it outputs location, the satellites available, and the signal strength, but more data can be usually found. Here, we just read the data and print it to the computer.

Code breakdown

First, we include the required `SoftwareSerial.h` library:

```
#include <SoftwareSerial.h>
```

Then we declare a `SoftwareSerial` port:

```
SoftwareSerial softSerial(8, 9); // RX, TX
```

We begin both serial connections in the `setup()` function:

```
void setup(){
  Serial.begin(9600); // Normal Serial
  softSerial.begin(9600); // Soft Serial
}
```

In the `loop()` function, we check whether there is any character available on the soft serial. If there is, we directly send it to the real serial port, which is connected to the computer. This basically makes Arduino a wire that transfers all the data from the GPS to the computer:

```
if (softSerial.available()){
    Serial.write(softSerial.read());
}
```

If we run the code now, with the GPS connected, we will see quite a bit of data in the serial monitor. The GPS will print the longitude, latitude, number of satellites found, and the signal strength. More details may be printed if available and depending on the GPS module.

Using the Copernicus module inside a thick building, the Arduino continuously printed:

`$GPGGA,,5316.82829,N,08650.76721,W,7,03,,,,,,,*4E`

This represents `53.1682829` latitude with 8.65207672 longitude, which corresponds to North Bremen, Germany. It also shows that three satellites are available and the signal quality is around 7.

There's more...

The Arduino can actually use the data from the GPS. With some string manipulation, we can extract the longitude and latitude and use it for localization or navigation purposes. For example, we can build an autonomous boat into which we input the GPS coordinates of a large lake, and the boat can travel there by checking the difference between the current location and the destination. Check the *See also* section for further references about string manipulation.

See also

► To learn how GPS triangulation works, visit `http://electronics.howstuffworks.com/gadgets/travel/gps.htm`

► For more details about Arduino string manipulation, visit `http://arduino.cc/en/Reference/StrsingObject`

5
Motor Control

In this chapter, we will cover the following topics:

- ▸ Controlling small motors
- ▸ Controlling motors with transistors
- ▸ Controlling speed with PWM
- ▸ Spinning motors both ways
- ▸ Servo motor
- ▸ Stepper motor
- ▸ Bipolar stepper motor
- ▸ Brushless motor

Introduction

This chapter deals with common types of motors and how they can be operated with Arduino. While making an LED blink or showing some text on a screen can be cool, nothing is more powerful than making something move. Here, we will tackle most of the types of motor that we can find these days.

There are many things that can be done using motors. Using a simple servo motor, we can position things precisely. For example, a robotic hand is usually just a bunch of servo motors glued together. By using a few standard DC motors, we can make a car move, make a robot turn, or make a boat move forward.

We will explore standard DC motors, servo motors, stepper motors, and brushless motors in this chapter.

Controlling small motors

Controlling a small motor can be very simple. If the motor is small enough, it can be directly connected to the Arduino pin, and simply turning the pin to HIGH or LOW will control the motor.

This recipe will teach you the basic logic of how to control a motor; however, this is not a typical way of connecting a motor to the Arduino. It is recommended that you first understand this recipe and then apply the following one, *Controlling motors with transistors*.

Getting ready

Following are the ingredients required to execute this recipe:

▸ An Arduino board connected to a computer via USB

▸ A 220-ohm resistor

▸ A very small DC motor—usually a vibration motor will work—that can be found in old (and new) mobile phones or can typically be brought from websites such as Sparkfun or Adafruit

How to do it...

The following are the steps to connect the motor:

1. Just like other small motors, a vibration motor has two wires. Connect one wire to the Arduino **GND** pin. It doesn't matter which one, as a DC motor has no polarity; it can be connected both ways.

2. Mount the resistor between the chosen digital pin and the remaining wire on the motor. The resistor will limit the current and ensure that the Arduino will not burn. Arduino is not really designed to drive motors this way.

Schematic

This is one possible implementation on the second digital pin. Other digital pins can be also be used.

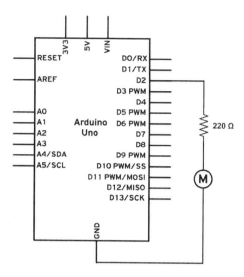

Here is an example of how to wire it on a breadboard:

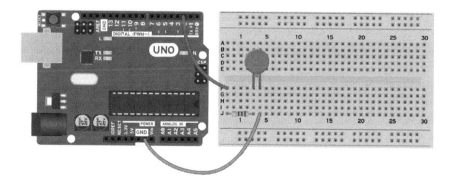

Code

The following code will start the motor for 1 second and then stop it for another:

```
// Declare the pin for the motor
int motorPin = 2;

void setup() {
  // Define pin #2 as output
  pinMode(motorPin, OUTPUT);

}
```

```
void loop(){
    // Turn motor on
    digitalWrite(motorPin, HIGH);
    // Wait 1000 ms
    delay(1000);
    // Turn motor off
    digitalWrite(motorPin, LOW);
    // Wait another 1000 ms
    delay(1000);
}
```

If the motor is connected on a different pin, simply change the `motorPin` value to the value of the pin that has been used.

How it works...

Whenever we set the pin at HIGH, current will flow from the digital pin through the resistor, through the motor, and to ground. If the motor is small enough, it will start spinning if it's a standard DC motor; else it will start vibrating, if it is a vibration motor.

The resistor is very important in this circuit. Each Arduino digital pin can only handle up to 40 mA, with 20 mA as the recommended maximum. The chosen 220-ohm value will limit the current to 22 mA, and because the motor is in series with another resistor, the current will be less. If the total resistance of the motor is higher than 200 Ohms then it's safe to omit the resistor and directly connect the motor to the digital pin and GND.

There's more...

In this example, we've seen how to connect one motor directly to a digital pin. But we can also connect more than one.

Multiple motors

Multiple motors can be connected using different digital pins on the Arduino board. For example, pins 2, 3, and 4 can independently control different motors. Each digital pin on the Arduino can control one motor. However, it's generally advised not to do this, as it will increase the current passing through the Arduino until it burns. Let's limit ourselves to one motor only with this implementation.

Electrical spikes

Every DC motor is also an inductor. When we stop supplying the motor with current, or when we spin the motor by hand, it will generate high-voltage electric spikes. This can easily burn electronic components. To avoid this, we should connect a diode from the digital pin to 5V, with the diode pointing to 5V. Whenever the motor generates a spike, the diode will pass it to the 5V line, which can tolerate it. Luckily, the Arduino has a built-in protection diode on each pin.

See also

- ▶ The *Controlling motors with transistors* recipe
- ▶ The *Controlling speed* with PWM recipe
- ▶ The *Spinning motors both ways* recipe

- ▶ To find out more about the digital pins of the Arduino, take a look at the I/O-Ports section in the ATMega328P microcontroller, found in Arduino Uno at `http://www.atmel.com/images/Atmel-8271-8-bit-AVR-Microcontroller-ATmega48A-48PA-88A-88PA-168A-168PA-328-328P_datasheet_Complete.pdf`

- ▶ To learn in detail how a DC motor works, visit `http://electronics.howstuffworks.com/motor.htm`

Controlling motors with transistors

We can control a motor by directly connecting it to the Arduino digital pin; however, any motor bigger than a coin would kill the digital pin and most probably burn Arduino. The solution is to use a simple amplification device, the transistor, to aid in controlling motors of any size.

Here, we will explore how to control larger motors using both NPN and PNP transistors.

Getting ready

To execute this recipe, you will require the following ingredients:

- ▶ An Arduino board connected to a computer via USB
- ▶ A DC motor
- ▶ A resistor between 220 ohm and 10K ohm
- ▶ A standard NPN transistor (BC547, 2N3904, N2222A, TIP120)
- ▶ A standard diode (1N4148, 1N4001, 1N4007)

All these components can be found on websites such as Adafruit, Pololu, and Sparkfun, or in any general electronics store.

How to do it...

The following are the steps to connect a motor using a transistor:

1. Connect the Arduino **GND** to the long strip on the breadboard.

2. Connect one of the motor terminals to VIN or **5V** on the Arduino. We use 5V if we power the board from the USB port. If we want higher voltages, we could use an external power source, such as a battery, and connect it to the power jack on Arduino. However, even the power jack has an input voltage range of 7 V–12 V. Don't exceed these limitations.

3. Connect the other terminal of the motor to the collector pin on the NPN transistor. Check the datasheet to identify which terminal on the transistor is the collector.

4. Connect the emitter pin of the **NPN** transistor to the **GND** using the long strip or a long connection.

5. Mount a resistor between the base pin of the NPN transistor and one digital pin on the Arduino board.

6. Mount a protection diode in parallel with the motor. The diode should point to 5V if the motor is powered by 5V, or should point to VIN if we use an external power supply.

Schematic

This is one possible implementation on the ninth digital pin. The Arduino has to be powered by an external supply. If not, we can connect the motor to 5V and it will be powered with 5 volts.

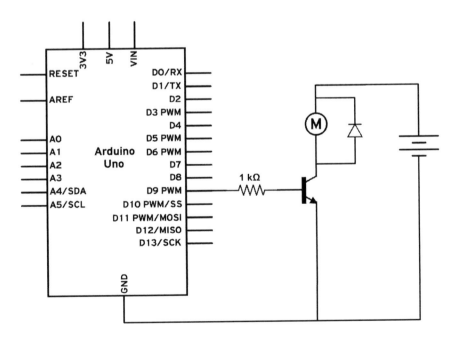

Here is one way of hooking up the motor and the transistor on a breadboard:

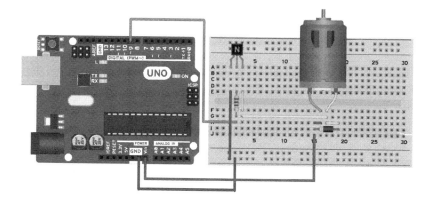

Code

For the coding part, nothing changes if we compare it with a small motor directly mounted on the pin. The code will start the motor for 1 second and then stop it for another one:

```
// Declare the pin for the motor
int motorPin = 2;


void setup() {
  // Define pin #2 as output
  pinMode(motorPin, OUTPUT);

}

void loop(){
  // Turn motor on
  digitalWrite(motorPin, HIGH);
  // Wait 1000 ms
  delay(1000);
  // Turn motor off
  digitalWrite(motorPin, LOW);
  // Wait another 1000 ms
  delay(1000);
}
```

 If the motor is connected to a different pin, simply change the motorPin value to the value of the pin that has been used.

How it works...

Transistors are very neat components that are unfortunately hard to understand. We should think of a transistor as an electric valve: the more current we put into the valve, the more water it will allow to flow. The same happens with a transistor; only here, current flows. If we apply a current on the base of the transistor, a proportional current will be allowed to pass from the collector to the emitter, in the case of an NPN transistor. The more current we put on the base, the more the flow of current will be between the other two terminals.

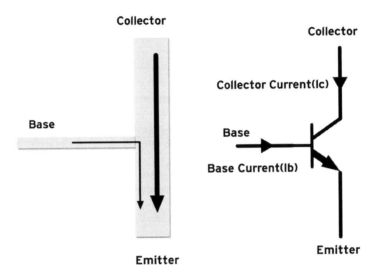

When we set the digital pin at HIGH on the Arduino, current passes from the pin to the base of the NPN transistor, thus allowing current to pass through the other two terminals. When we set the pin at LOW, no current goes to the base and so, no current will pass through the other two terminals. Another analogy would be a digital switch that allows current to pass from the collector to the emitter only when we 'push' the base with current.

Transistors are very useful because, with a very small current on the base, we can control a very large current from the collector to the emitter. A typical amplification factor called β for a transistor is 200. This means that, for a base current of 1 mA, the transistor will allow a maximum of 200 mA to pass from the collector to the emitter.

An important component is the diode, which should never be omitted. A motor is also an inductor; whenever an inductor is cut from power it may generate large voltage spikes, which could easily destroy a transistor. The diode makes sure that all current coming out of the motor goes back to the power supply and not to the motor.

There's more...

Transistors are handy devices; here are a few more things that can be done with them.

Pull-down resistor

The base of a transistor is very sensitive. Even touching it with a finger might make the motor turn. A solution to avoid unwanted noise and starting the motor is to use a pull-down resistor on the base pin, as shown in the following figure. A value of around 10K is recommended, and it will safeguard the transistor from accidentally starting.

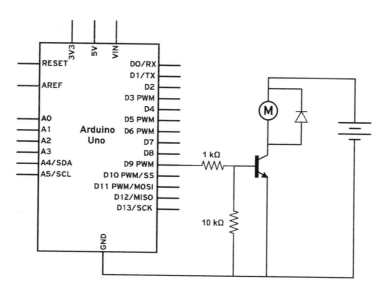

PNP transistors

A PNP transistor is even harder to understand. It uses the same principle, but in reverse. Current flows from the base to the digital pin on the Arduino; if we allow that current to flow, the transistor will allow current to pass from its emitter to its collector (yes, the opposite of what happens with an NPN transistor). Another important point is that the PNP is mounted between the power source and the load we want to power up. The load, in this case a motor, will be connected between the collector on the PNP and the ground.

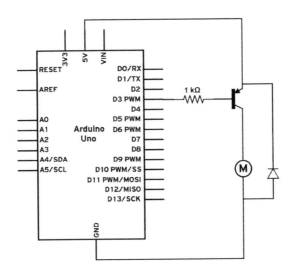

A key point to remember while using PNP transistors with Arduino is that the maximum voltage on the emitter is 5 V, so the motor will never receive more than 5 V. If we use an external power supply for the motor, the base will have a voltage higher than 5 V and will burn the Arduino. One possible solution, which is quite complicated, has been shown here:

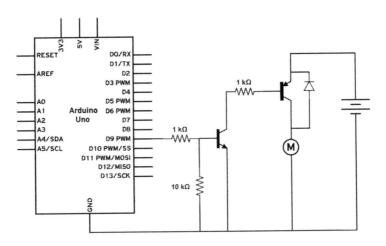

MOSFETs

Let's face it; NPN and PNP transistors are old. There are better things these days that can provide much better performance. They are called Metal-oxide-semiconductor field-effect transistors. Normal people just call them MOSFETs and they work mostly the same. The three pins on a normal transistor are called collector, base, and emitter. On the MOSFET, they are called drain, gate, and source. Operation-wise, we can use them exactly the same way as with normal transistors. When voltage is applied at the gate, current will pass from the drain to the source in the case of an N-channel MOSFET. A P-channel is the equivalent of a PNP transistor.

However, there are some important differences in the way a MOSFET works compared with a normal transistor. Not all MOSFETs can be properly powered on by the Arduino. Usually logic-level MOSFETs will work. Some of the famous N-channel MOSFETs are the FQP30N06, the IRF510, and the IRF520. The first one can handle up to 30 A and 60 V while the following two can handle 5.6 A and 10 A, respectively, at 100 V.

Here is one implementation of the previous circuit, this time using an N-channel MOSFET:

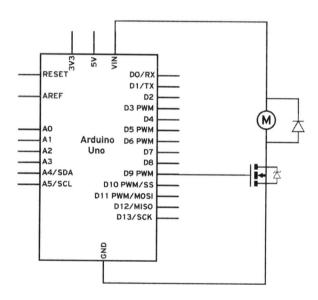

We can also use the following breadboard arrangement:

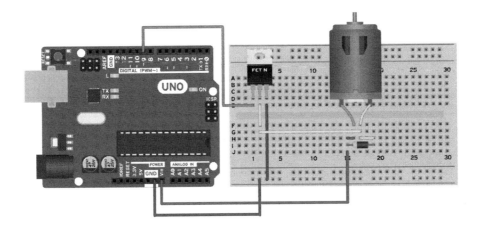

Different loads

A motor is not the only thing we can control with a transistor. Any kind of DC load can be controlled. An LED, a light or other tools, even another Arduino can be powered up by an Arduino and a PNP or NPN transistor. Arduinoception!

See also

▸ The *Controlling speed with PWM* recipe.

▸ For general and easy to use motors, Solarbotics is quite nice. Visit the site at `https://solarbotics.com/catalog/motors-servos/`.

▸ For higher-end motors that pack quite some power, Pololu has made a name for itself. Visit the site at `https://www.pololu.com/category/51/pololu-metal-gearmotors`.

Controlling speed with PWM

A motor that can only be on or off is not that useful. We need to control the speed of a motor using code. Sometimes, we want the motor at half speed; sometimes we want it faster and sometimes slower. However, the motor is connected to a digital pin, whose value can either be maximum or nothing. How can we make this clear 1 and 0 into something in-between? With Pulse Width Modulation or PWM.

Getting ready

Following are the ingredients needed for this recipe:

- A DC motor
- A resistor between 220 ohm and 4,700 ohm
- A standard NPN transistor (BC547, 2N3904, N2222A, TIP120) or a logic-level compatible MOSFET (IRF510, IRF520)
- A standard diode (1N4148, 1N4001, 1N4007)

How to do it...

The following are the steps to control the speed of a motor using PWM:

1. Connect the Arduino **GND** to the long strip on the breadboard.

2. Connect one of the motor terminals to VIN or **5V** on the Arduino. We use 5V if we power the board from the USB port or, if we want higher voltages, we could use an external power source, such as a battery, and connect it to the power jack on the Arduino.

3. Connect the other terminal of the motor to the collector pin on the NPN transistor or to the drain pin on the MOSFET. Check the datasheet to identify which terminal on the transistor is the collector or which terminal on the MOSFET is the drain.

4. Connect the emitter pin of the NPN transistor or the source pin of the MOSFET to the GND using the long strip or a long connection.

5. Mount a resistor between the base or gate pin of the transistor and one PWM pin on the Arduino. These pins are generally marked with ~ next to the pin number on the board. The Arduino Uno has pins 3, 5, 6, 9, 10, and 11 as PWM pins.

6. Mount a protection diode in parallel with the motor terminals, pointing to either VIN or 5V, depending on whether an external power supply has been used or not.

Schematic

This is one possible implementation. Other digital pins with PWM functionality can be used; in this example, the ninth digital pin has been used:

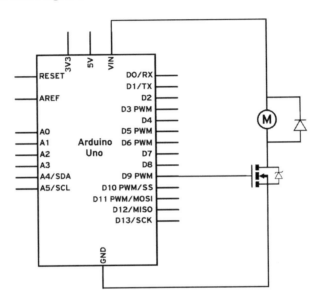

Here is a possible breadboard implementation:

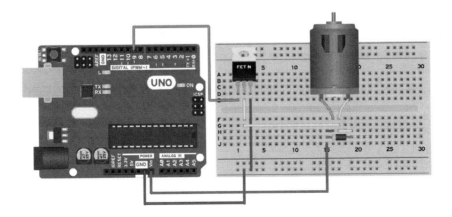

Code

The following code will start the motor at maximum speed and then gradually reduce its speed until it stops it:

```
// Declare the pin for the motor
int motorPin = 9;

void setup() {
  // PWM pins don't require the pinMode() function
}

void loop(){
  // Turn motor on to maximum
  analogWrite(motorPin, 255);
  // Wait 1000 ms
  delay(1000);

  // Turn motor to 1/2 power
  analogWrite(motorPin, 127);
  // Wait 1000 ms
  delay(1000);

  // Turn motor off
  analogWrite(motorPin, 0);
  // Wait 1000 ms
  delay(1000);
}
```

 If the motor is connected to a different pin, simply change the `motorPin` value to the value of the pin that has been used. However, it has to be a PWM-enabled pin.

How it works...

PWM is a clever trick that allows a digital pin, which can only output 1 or 0, to simulate values in-between. It works by switching the digital pin on and off very fast. For example, if we switch a digital pin on for 1 millisecond and off for another millisecond, we will be doing this on-off cycle 500 times a second. If we have a motor connected to the pin, the motor will spin at half speed. Why? Because, first of all, we are actually giving it power half of the time, since the pin is off for 1 millisecond every 2 milliseconds.

In practice, this means we are turning it on and off, but due to the high frequency at which we are doing it, the result will be a motor with half power. This, of course, doesn't work at low frequencies. If we turn the motor on for a second and off for another one, the result will be a motor that is truly starting and stopping; so, the higher the frequency, the better.

This doesn't mean that we can only have half-speed. By varying the time that it is on and the time it is off, we can obtain many speed variations. And the best part is that the Arduino has an inbuilt library to handle this. The following diagram shows how all of this works in a more graphic way:

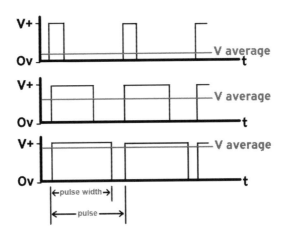

We can see in the first part of the graphic that we are mostly keeping the pin LOW, to 0 V, and thus the average voltage output is quite low. In the middle of the graphic, we are roughly keeping the pin HIGH and LOW for an equal amount of time, and the resulting voltage is half. In the last part, we see that the time the pin is HIGH is called Pulse Width. The total time between the beginning of each pulse is called the period of the PWM signal.

A few pins on the Arduino are PWM-enabled and can be used to generate this PWM signal. On almost all Arduinos, the PWM pins are 3, 5, 6, 9, 10, and 11. The exceptions are the Arduino Due and Mega, which have more PWMs on pins 2 to 13.

Almost all Arduinos can output 8-bit PWM signals at a frequency of 490 Hz Exceptions are the newer boards such as the Uno that, for pins 5 and 6, output 980 Hz. An 8-bit PWM means that we can output a level between 0, which is the equivalent of LOW, up to 255, which is the equivalent of HIGH. The middle is roughly at 127.

Code breakdown

The code uses the `analogWrite()` function, which outputs a PWM signal on a PWM-enabled pin, at the specified level:

```
analogWrite(motorPin, 127);
```

This function will output the PWM signal at the value of `127`, which is roughly half of the 0–255 range. Other values can be provided, such as 85 for one-third and 170 for two-thirds.

A very good thing to remember is that the `analogWrite()` function used on PWM-compatible pins will not use the processor continuously. Once we call `analogWrite()` at a specific level, the code execution will continue and the PWM signal will be generated continuously, until stopped. This is a very good thing because we can leave all PWM at the levels we want and then execute the rest of the code with no interruption.

There's more...

The PWM pins are very useful. Any load can be controlled with them; for example, LED intensity, motors, or speakers. In order to use multiple PWM pins, in the `analogWrite()` pin value, we just need to modify the pin argument to the pin we want to change.

Spinning motors both ways

It's very simple to control a motor with a transistor. However, spinning the motor in just one direction is not always that useful. It's just half of what is possible. Most DC motors can spin both ways. When we apply the voltage in one direction, the motor will spin on one side. If we reverse the voltage on the terminals, the motor will spin the opposite way. But how can we do that with the Arduino? We need to use an H-Bridge.

Getting ready

Following are the ingredients required for this recipe:

- An Arduino board connected to a computer via USB
- An Arduino-compatible motor shield; there is an official Arduino motor shield and a few other options from different companies such as Sparkfun, Pololu, or Adafruit
- A DC motor

How to do it...

Arduino shields are very useful because they can simply be plugged into the Arduino and everything is already made. We don't need to spend a lot of time routing wires to breadboards and testing. Everything just works.

The following are the steps to connect a motor using a motor shield:

1. Plug the motor shield into the Arduino.
2. Connect the two wire terminals of the motor to one of the motor terminal ports.

Here is a schematic of the logical connections needed between the Arduino and the shield. In this example, we are only using two of the six pins to control one motor.

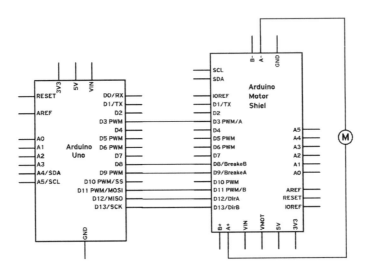

This is a view of the shield connected to the motor and the motor connected to the shield:

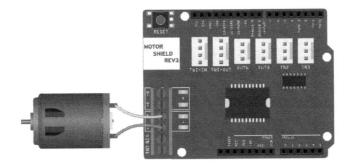

Code

The following code will define a motor control function and will use it to spin the motor forward at half speed, full speed, and then stop; the motor will then reverse at half speed, reverse at full speed, and stop again:

```
// Declare the used pins
int directionPin = 12;
```

```
int pwmPin = 3;


void setup() {
  // Set the directionPin as OUTPUT
  pinMode(directionPin, OUTPUT);
  // PWM pins don't require the pinMode() function
}


// Custom function which controls the speed and direction using one
  variable.
void setMotor(int val){
  // If val is from 0 to 255 the motor will spin forwards
  if (val >= 0){
    // Set the direction
    digitalWrite(directionPin, HIGH);
    // Set the speed
    analogWrite(pwmPin, val);
  }
  // If the value is from -255 to 0 the motor will spin backwards
  if (val < 0){
    // Set the direction
    digitalWrite(directionPin, LOW);
    // Set the speed, -val because the value is negative and positive
    is requried
    analogWrite(pwmPin, -val);
  }
}


void loop(){
  // Turn motor on half speed forwards
  setMotor(127);
  delay(1000);

  // Motor full speed forwards
  setMotor(255);
  delay(1000);
  // Motor stop
  setMotor(0);
  delay(1000);

  // Motor half speed backwards
  setMotor(-127);
```

```
    delay(1000);

    // Motor full speed backwards
    setMotor(-255);
    delay(1000);

    // Motor stop
    setMotor(0);
    delay(1000);
}
```

 There are multiple types of motor shields for the Arduino. The presented code will only control one motor on the official Arduino Motor Shield. Variations have been provided in the *There's more...* section of this recipe.

How it works...

In order to spin a motor two ways, we need a circuit called the H-bridge. It is composed of four transistors that control the current direction through the motor. However, this circuit is quite complicated and it's very easy to accidentally burn it. The good news is that there are integrated circuits that already implement this H-bridge concept and add safety features such as short protection, over-current protection, and over-temperature shutdown.

For the purpose of this recipe, we will not discuss in depth how the H-bridge works; that will be covered in a further recipe. In fact, there are so many motor shields and motor drivers out there that most probably we will never need to implement a full H-bridge by ourselves.

However, there are some variations even in the shields that are commonly used. Some use only one pin to control the direction and speed of a motor, some use two, some three and some even four. Some drivers can handle one motor; some can handle two motors. Next, we will break down the code to control one motor on the Arduino Motor Driver Shield.

Code breakdown

The code defines the two pins required to control one motor. One is the direction pin, which sets the direction of the motor. When it is HIGH, the motor will spin one way, and when it is LOW, the other way. The other pin is the PWM pin that controls the speed of the motor. If, for example, we set the direction pin to HIGH and speed to 127, the motor will turn one direction with roughly half the speed. If we then change the direction pin to LOW, it will reverse its direction and maintain roughly half the speed.

In the `setup()` function, we declare `directionPin` as an output. PWM pins don't need to be declared:

```
void setup() {
  // Set the directionPin as OUTPUT
  pinMode(directionPin, OUTPUT);
  // PWM pins don't require the pinMode() function
}
```

The custom `setMotor()` function takes one argument: the speed of the motor. If the speed is between 0 and 255, the motor will spin forward with the respective speed. For 0, it will not move of course. If the value is from -1 to -255, the motor will spin backwards with a power of 1 to 255.

We do this using a simple `if` statement. If the value is over 0, we set the direction pin as HIGH and set the speed directly:

```
// Custom function which controls the speed and direction using one
variable
void setMotor(int val){
  // If val is from 0 to 255 the motor will spin forwards
  if (val >= 0){
    // Set the direction
    digitalWrite(directionPin, HIGH);
    // Set the speed
    analogWrite(pwmPin, val);
  }
```

But if the speed is negative, we set the direction pin as LOW and then we use a simple trick for the `analogWrite()` function. It doesn't accept negative values, but by putting a minus sign before the value, we reverse the sign. This way, `-val` will equal the positive part of `val` when `val` is negative:

```
// If the value is from -255 to 0 the motor will spin backwards
  if (val < 0){
    // Set the direction
    digitalWrite(directionPin, LOW);
    // Set the speed, -val because the value is negative and positive
    is requried
    analogWrite(pwmPin, -val);
  }
```

Then, in the `loop()` function, we just test our custom function by turning the motor in different directions. The comments explain best what is happening.

There's more...

The Arduino Motor Shield can control two motors at the same time. Also, it is not the only shield on the market that can control motors. Actually, there are hundreds of motor shields and motor drivers. They all share the same H-Bridge principle and so they are all controlled in similar ways. Here, we will explore a few typical configurations and understand how to adjust our `setMotor()` function to be compatible with other motors.

Control using the direction pin, PWM pin, and brake pin

The Arduino Motor Shield uses one direction and one PWM pin. And it is not the only one to do so; the Sparkfun Ardumoto shield has identical pin mappings. The pins are as follows:

Function	Pin for Motor A	Pin for Motor B
Direction pin	12	13
PWM pin	3	11
Brake pin	9	8

Now, what is the brake pin? The Arduino Motor Shield has this pin that, when turned HIGH, will stop the motor. We can adjust our `setMotor()` function with this new feature as follows:

```
void setMotor(int val){
  // If val is 0 braking will be applied
  if (val == 0){
    // Start braking
    digitalWrite(brakePin, HIGH);
  }
  // If val is from 1 to 255 the motor will spin forwards
  if (val > 0){
    // Set the direction
    digitalWrite(directionPin, HIGH);
    // Set the speed
    analogWrite(pwmPin, val);
    // Stop the braking
    digitalWrite(brakePin, LOW);
  }
  // If the value is from -255 to 0 the motor will spin backwards
  if (val < 0){
    // Set the direction
    digitalWrite(directionPin, LOW);
    // Set the speed, -val because the value is negative and positive
    is requried
    analogWrite(pwmPin, -val);
```

```
    // Stop the braking
    digitalWrite(brakePin, LOW);
  }
}
```

Now we can use the `setMotor()` function, and when we want to brake, we simply need to pass 0 as the motor speed.

Control using Input A, Input B, and PWM

There are so many variations, but this is a popular one. It uses two digital pins for direction and one for PWM. This only uses one PWM pin while the other two can be digital.

But how do we make the driver go forward, backward, or even brake? Here is a reference table:

Input A	Input B	Result
0	0	Low brake
0	1	Forward
1	0	Backward
1	1	High brake

High side and low side braking are interesting concepts. In high side braking, both motor terminals are connected to the power supply, while in low side braking, both are connected to ground. This will make the motor brake.

How do we control the speed? We can use the PWM input. With Input A and B, we set the direction, and with PWM, the speed. Now we can stop the motor by either sending a 0 or 11 on the AB pins, or by just writing 0 to the PWM. Here is our `setMotor()` function for this configuration:

```
void setMotor (int val){
  // If val is 0 braking will be applied
  if (val == 0){
    // Start braking
    digitalWrite(pinA, LOW);
    digitalWrite(pinB, LOW);
  }

  // If val is from 1 to 255 the motor will spin forwards
  if (val > 0){
    // Set the direction
    digitalWrite(pinA, LOW);
    digitalWrite(pinB, HIGH);
    // Set the speed
```

```
  analogWrite(pwmPin, val);
}
// If value is from -255 to -1 the motor will spin back
if (val < 0){
  // Set the direction
  digitalWrite(pinA, HIGH);
  digitalWrite(pinB, LOW);
  // Set the speed
  analogWrite(pwmPin, -val);
}
```

Some drivers also have an enable pin which we need to either set as HIGH or LOW in order to enable the motor. Sometimes, these drivers are actually missing the PWM pin but have an enable pin. By applying PWM to it, we can obtain the same result.

Custom-made L293D driver

This one is for the brave! We can build our own H-bridge driver using the famous L293D H-bridge driver. When we don't really have space, we can make our custom electronics board with the following schematic, which controls two motors:

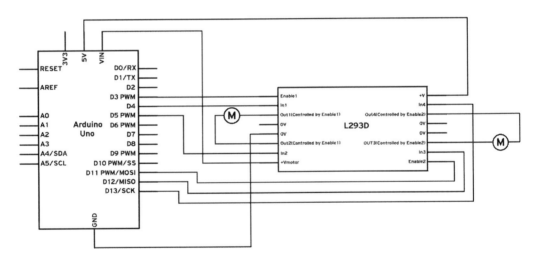

But if we want to implement it on the breadboard, this is one possible way:

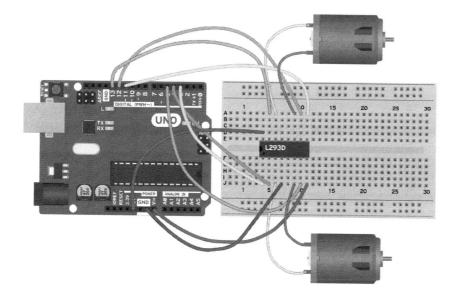

There is another **Integrated Circuit (IC)** that functions identical to L293D; heck, it even looks the same—all the pins are the same. It's a little cheaper, and it's called SN754410.

See also

▸   Whenever we are using an IC, we should check its datasheet. You can find the datasheet for L293D at http://www.ti.com/lit/ds/symlink/l293d.pdf

Servo motor

Servo motors are great devices that can turn to a specified position. Usually, they have a servo arm that can turn 180 degrees. Using the Arduino, we can tell a servo to go to a specified position and it will go there. As simple as that!

Servo motors were first used in the **Remote Control (RC)** world, usually to control the steering of RC cars or the flaps on a RC plane. With time, they found their uses in robotics, automation, and of course, the Arduino world.

Here we will see how to connect a servo motor26 and then how to turn it to different positions.

The first motor I ever connected to an Arduino, seven years ago, was a Servo motor. Nostalgic moment over, back to work!

Getting ready

For this recipe, you will need the following ingredients:

- An Arduino board connected to a computer via USB
- A servo motor
- Jumper wires

There are few big names in the servo motor world. Hiteh and Futaba are the leading RC servo manufacturers. Good places to buy them are Servocity, Sparkfun, and Hobbyking.

How to do it...

A servo motor has everything built in: a motor, a feedback circuit, and most important, a motor driver. It just needs one power line, one ground, and one control pin.

Following are the steps to connect a servo motor to the Arduino:

1. The servo motor has a female connector with three pins. The darkest or even black one is usually the ground. Connect this to the Arduino **GND**.
2. Connect the power cable that in all standards should be red to **5V** on the Arduino.
3. Connect the remaining line on the servo connector to a digital pin on the Arduino.

This is a view of the servo motor connected to the Arduino:

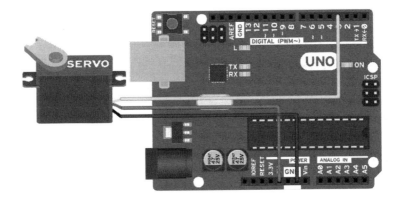

Code

The following code will turn a servo motor to 0 degrees, wait 1 second, then turn it to 90, wait one more second, turn it to 180, and then go back.

```
// Include the Servo library
#include <Servo.h>

// Declare the Servo pin
int servoPin = 3;
// Create a servo object
Servo Servo1;

void setup() {
  // We need to attach the servo to the used pin number
  Servo1.attach(servoPin);
}

void loop(){
  // Make servo go to 0 degrees
  Servo1.write(0);
  delay(1000);
  // Make servo go to 90 degrees
  Servo1.write(90);
  delay(1000);
  // Make servo go to 180 degrees
  Servo1.write(180);
  delay(1000);
}
```

 If the servo motor is connected on another digital pin, simply change the value of servoPin to the value of the digital pin that has been used.

How it works...

Servos are clever devices. Using just one input pin, they receive the position from the Arduino and they go there. Internally, they have a motor driver and a feedback circuit that makes sure that the servo arm reaches the desired position. But what kind of signal do they receive on the input pin?

It is a square wave similar to PWM. Each cycle in the signal lasts for 20 milliseconds and for most of the time, the value is LOW. At the beginning of each cycle, the signal is HIGH for a time between 1 and 2 milliseconds. At 1 millisecond it represents 0 degrees and at 2 milliseconds it represents 180 degrees. In between, it represents the value from 0–180. This is a very good and reliable method. The following graphic makes it a little easier to understand:

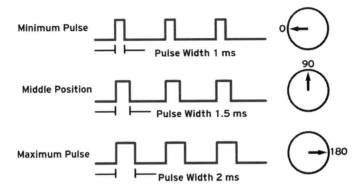

Remember that using the `Servo` library automatically disables PWM functionality on PWM pins 9 and 10 on the Arduino UNO and similar boards.

Code breakdown

The code simply declares the servo object and then initializes the servo by using the `servo.attach()` function. We shouldn't forget to include the servo library. In the `loop()`, we set the servo to 0 degrees, wait, then set it to 90, and later to 180 degrees.

There's more...

Controlling servos is easy, and here are a few more tricks we can use.

Controlling the exact pulse time

Arduino has a built-in function `servo.write(degrees)` that simplifies the control of servos. However, not all servos respect the same timings for all positions. Usually, 1 millisecond means 0 degrees, 1.5 milliseconds mean 90 degrees, and, of course, 2 milliseconds mean 180 degrees. Some servos have smaller or larger ranges.

For better control, we can use the `servo.writeMicroseconds(us)` function, which takes the exact number of microseconds as a parameter. Remember, 1 millisecond equals 1,000 microseconds.

More servos

In order to use more than one servo, we need to declare multiple servo objects, attach different pins to each one, and address each servo individually.

First, we need to declare the servo objects—as many as we need:

```
// Create servo objects
Servo Servo1, Servo2, Servo3;
```

Then we need to attach each object to one servo motor. Remember, every servo motor uses an individual pin:

```
Servo1.attach(servoPin1);
Servo2.attach(servoPin2);
Servo3.attach(servoPin3);
```

In the end, we just have to address each servo object individually:

```
Servo1.write(0);   // Set Servo 1 to 0 degrees
Servo2.write(90);  // Set Servo 2 to 90 degrees
```

Connection-wise, the grounds from the servos go to GND on the Arduino, the servo power to 5V or VIN (depending on the power input), and in the end, each signal line has to be connected to a different digital pin. Contrary to popular belief, servos don't need to be controlled by PWM pins—any digital pin will work.

Continuous rotation servos

There is a special breed of servos labelled as **continuous rotation servos**. While a normal servo goes to a specific position depending on the input signal, a continuous rotation servo either rotates clockwise or counter-clockwise at a speed proportional to the signal. For example, the `Servo1.write(0)` function will make the servomotor spin counter-clockwise at full speed. The `Servo1.write(90)` function will stop the motor and `Servo1.write(180)` will turn the motor clockwise at full speed.

There are multiple uses for such servos; however, they are really slow. If you are building a microwave and need a motor to turn the food, this is your choice. But be careful, microwaves are dangerous!

See also

A servo motor offers ease of use with high precision and power. However, there are other motor types offering the same and they even have full continuous rotation. The *Stepper motor* recipe talks about them in detail.

Stepper motor

When we need precision and repeatability, a stepper motor is always the solution. With the way it is designed, a stepper can only move from one step to the next and fix in that position. A typical motor has 200 steps per revolution; if we tell the motor to go 100 steps in one direction, it will turn exactly 180 degrees. It gets interesting when we only tell it to go one step and it turns exactly 1.8 degrees.

Stepper motors are found in printers, scanners, industrial robot arms, 3D printers, and pretty much in every precision motion device.

There are two types of stepper motors: unipolar and bipolar. Unipolar motors are easier to control while bipolar motors are more powerful.

In this recipe, we will see how to connect a unipolar stepper motor using a common integrated circuit.

Getting ready

The following are the ingredients required to execute this recipe:

- An Arduino board connected to a computer via USB.
- A breadboard and jumper wires
- A unipolar stepper motor.
- A ULN2003A or ULN2004 Darlington Array Integrated Circuit. Just remember ULN2003A or ULN2004; they are basically seven transistors stacked together in a convenient package.

We can typically buy Stepper motors from Sparkfun, Pololu, Adafruit, common electronics stores, or even take them out from old printers.

How to do it...

We implement a simple circuit in which we only need the Arduino, the ULN IC on a breadboard, and the Unipolar stepper motor, in the following manner:

1. Connect the Arduino **GND** to a long strip on the breadboard.
2. Connect the ULN2003 or the ULN2004 to the center of the breadboard.
3. Connect pins 1 to 4—the first four pins on the left of the IC—to four digital pins on the Arduino.

4. The stepper motor has six wires. Two are the center of each winding. We need to identify these centers. The simplest way is to take a multimeter and use the resistance mode. Since the center pin is between two identical windings, it has to give an equal resistance with either one. So if we test all cable combinations, when we find a wire with equal resistance to the other two, we have found a center. When we find both, we connect them together to pin **9** on the IC.

5. We connect the other four cables on the stepper directly to the output of the IC; in this case, pins 13 to 16.

6. Now we need to connect the power supply. If we power the stepper from the built-in 5V, we connect **5V** to the common pin—pin **9** on the IC. If we use an external power supply, we can connect the positive terminal there or connect pin 9 to the VIN, if the Arduino is powered from an external power supply.

7. Lastly, we connect ground to the IC. Connect the **0V** pin, pin **8** to the **GND** strip we made earlier in step 1.

Schematic

This is one possible implementation. Other pins can also be used. The COM pin can be connected to 5V or an external power supply.

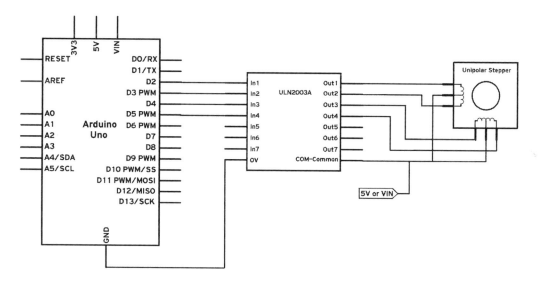

Here is a possible breadboard implementation:

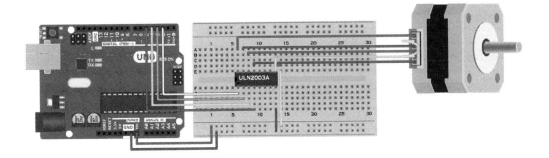

Code

The following code will spin a unipolar stepper 180 degrees in one direction and then back:

```
// Include the Stepper library
#include <Stepper.h>

// Declare a Stepper motor with 200 steps
// connected on pins 2,3,4,5
// Syntax:stepper1(stepsPerRevolution,pin1,pin2,pin3,pin4)
Stepper stepper1(200, 2, 3, 4, 5);

void setup() {
  // Set the speed of the stepper in RPM
  stepper1.setSpeed(60);
}

void loop(){
  // Turn the stepper 100 steps which means 180 degrees
  stepper1.step(100);
  // Wait half second
  delay(500);

  // Turn the stepper 100 steps back
  stepper1.step(-100);
  // Wait half second
  delay(500);
}
```

Other digital pins can be used when declaring the stepper motor. Also, other speeds can be tried. However, keep in mind that stepper motors are not very good with speed.

How it works...

Stepper motors differ from normal DC motors in that, rather than just spinning in one direction or another, they move in small increments in a given direction. These small increments are called steps. We can tell a stepper to go one or more steps in one particular direction. They are not necessarily fast, but they have high precision and quite some torque. For example, the paper feeder on a printer uses a stepper motor. 3D printers and CNC machines use them for very high precision and repeatability.

Luckily, the Arduino has a built-in library to control unipolar stepper motors. And they are very easy to control indeed.

Code breakdown

The code declares a stepper motor, selects a speed, and makes it turn in both directions.

Here, we declare the stepper motor. The syntax requires the number of steps of the motor as the first parameter and then the four pins to which we connected the motor:

```
Stepper stepper1(200, 2, 3, 4, 5);
```

Another important step is declaring the speed at which we want the motor to turn. If, for example, we set a speed of 60 RPM as in this case, and the motor has 200 steps, it will take around 5 milliseconds to increment one step. The speed of the motor can be changed at any time.

```
stepper1.setSpeed(60);}
```

Lastly, to make the motor move, we need to order the number of steps to increment. If we feed a negative number of steps, it will move in the opposite direction. Note that the step() function will pause the execution of the program until the motor spins completely. If, for example, we set 200 steps at a speed of 1 RPM, it will take one full minute until the Arduino will continue execution.

```
stepper1.step(-100);
```

 Arduino assumes the stepper moves while it orders it to move. The stepper has no feedback circuit, so if we hold the shaft of the motor, the Arduino will believe it is moving though the stepper might not be moving.

There's more...

The ULN2003A and ULN2004 integrated circuits are very useful little devices, especially when we control unipolar stepper motors, as they have everything built in—the transistor, the diode, and everything else. However, if it's really needed, we can just use four transistors, four diodes, and four resistors to spin a unipolar motor.

Transistor unipolar stepper driver

Here is one possible implementation of a custom unipolar stepper driver. We can use any standard NPN transistor. Darlington pairs are preferred, such as the TIP120, TIP121, or 2N6045. Remember that stepper motors use quite a lot of current, usually in the range of 2–5 A, so the chosen transistor has to be able to handle it. Here is one recommended implementation:

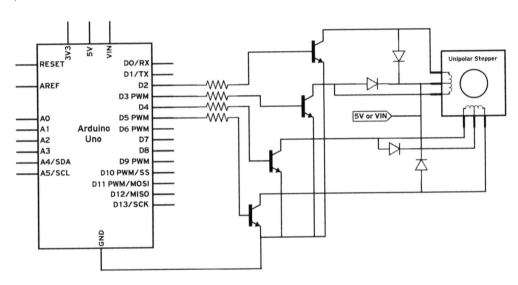

Identifying the stepper motor type

There are multiple stepper motor technologies. This is a simple guide on identifying the type. A four-cable stepper motor is usually bipolar. With six cables, it is most probably unipolar where the two center coil cables have to be connected together. There are some versions with only five cables that are also unipolar and already have the two center coils connected together internally. Also, there are stepper motors with eight cables, but they are incredibly rare. They are also unipolar and the four center cables have to be connected together.

See also

▶ Find a comprehensive tutorial on stepper motors at `https://learn.adafruit.com/all-about-stepper-motors/what-is-a-stepper-motor`

Bipolar stepper motors

Unipolar stepper motors are easy to control at the cost of low efficiency and power. Bipolar stepper motors have much higher efficiency and torque; however they are much harder to control. To fully control one, two H-bridges are required. Luckily there are multiple Arduino-compatible bipolar stepper drivers out there. Here we will explore a few options.

Getting ready

We can control a bipolar stepper motor using the Arduino Motor Shield. Here are the ingredients needed for this recipe:

- An Arduino board connected to a computer via USB
- An Arduino Motor Shield
- A bipolar stepper motor

How to do it...

We connect the stepper motor to the shield using the following steps:

1. Carefully mount the Arduino Motor Shield on top of the Arduino. Be careful not to bend any pins.
2. Identify the two coils. Use a multimeter to measure the resistance between all the wires. The ones with a low resistance in between are the coils.
3. Connect the four stepper wires to the main terminal output of the Shield. One coil goes to one motor output and the other one to the other output.

Here's how it should look:

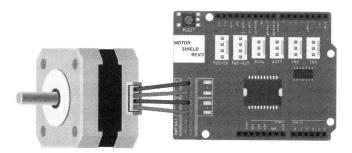

Code

The following code will spin the stepper motor 100 steps in one direction and 100 steps in the other:

```
// Include the Stepper library
#include <Stepper.h>

// Declare the used pins
int dirA = 12;
int dirB = 13;
int pwmA = 3;
int pwmB = 11;

// Declare a Stepper motor with 200 steps
Stepper stepper1(200, dirA, dirB);

void setup() {
  // PWM pins require declaration when used as Digital
  pinMode(pwmA, OUTPUT);
  pinMode(pwmB, OUTPUT);
  // Set PWM pins as always HIGH
  digitalWrite(pwmA, HIGH);
  digitalWrite(pwmB, HIGH);

  // Set stepper motor speed
  stepper1.setSpeed(60);
}

void loop(){
  // Turn the stepper 100 steps which means 180 degrees
  stepper1.step(100);
  // Wait half second
  delay(500);

  // Turn the stepper 100 steps back
  stepper1.step(-100);
  // Wait half second
  delay(500);
}
```

How it works...

A bipolar stepper motor only has two coils with no center tap, in contrast to a unipolar design. This means that the coils have to be turned on in both directions at different times. As a comparison, a bipolar stepper is exactly like two DC motors which always have to be controlled in the opposite direction at the same time. When one coil is excited in one direction, the other one has to be reversed. By shifting this, we generate a pulse which makes the stepper spin.

Code breakdown

Only the differences from the previous unipolar stepper recipe will be explained here. The code will do the same—it will turn the motor 100 steps in one direction and then in reverse.

We only need to declare the two direction pins of the Arduino Motor Shield. As explained in the *Spinning motors both ways* recipe, the direction pin sets which direction the coil will be excited in.

```
Stepper stepper1(200, dirA, dirB);
```

The two PWM pins select how much power we attribute to the coils. However, as this is a stepper, we always want full power; so we will simplify and directly set the PWM pins always as HIGH:

```
// PWM pins require declaration when used as Digital
pinMode(pwmA, OUTPUT);
pinMode(pwmB, OUTPUT);

// Set PWM pins as always HIGH
digitalWrite(pwmA, HIGH);
digitalWrite(pwmB, HIGH);
```

There's more...

Bipolar steppers are the most common breed. They are highly efficient and powerful at the price of having complex drivers. And there are a lot of drivers for them, way too many to be covered. Each one has a different input type. The best advice is to check a few well-known stepper driver producers such as Sparkfun, Pololu, or Adafruit. They offer guides for each of their stepper drivers, and these are usually very easy to use.

Brushless motors

Let's talk a little about the edge of electric motors. A typical electric motor has a rotor, a stator, and brushes. The brushes transmit the electrical current to the rotor, thus spinning the motor. The drawback of the brushes is that they continuously rub on the commutator. As an analogy, imagine driving a car with the breaks partially pressed. That's what the brushes do to the motor. However, there is a solution!

Brushless motors, as the name implies, do not have any brushes. This means they are much more efficient, they last longer, and they are more powerful. But of course there is a drawback; they require complicated control. Luckily, brushless motors have found their way into the remote-controlled world and we can now find cheap and useful brushless motors and brushless motor controllers or **Electronic Speed Control** (**ESC**).

Getting ready

To make this recipe work, we will need a few basic things:

▸ An Arduino board connected to a computer via USB.

▸ An RC brushless motor, which is available in two types—inrunners and outrunners. Inrunners look similar to a normal DC motor but they run at very high speeds, while outrunners are wider and shorter, and—wait for it—their case rotates, not the center of the motor. Isn't that strange? We can find brushless motors in any RC model store. Some famous stores they are sold in are Conrad for Europe and Hobbyking for USA and worldwide.

▸ A brushless motor driver or ESC, Careful! There are ESCs for standard DC motors—not many—but there are. A quick way to determine if an ESC is for brushless motors (other than reading the description) is to check how many output cables it has. If it has three cables, it is for brushless motors. Otherwise, keep searching. They can be found at any store that sells brushless motors.

How to do it...

A brushless motor driver uses the same standard connector and signal as an RC servo. Here are the steps to connect everything:

1. Connect the three wires of the motor to the three output wires of the ESC.

2. The ESC needs power, and brushless motors are very hungry! It is recommended to use a lithium-ion or lithium polymer battery, designed for high loads, in order to control such motors. Don't be misled by the 9 V battery in the graphic.

3. Lastly, connect the control wire to the Arduino. Remember, ESCs use the same standard connector and signal as any RC servo. We may omit the red, 5V connection, as ESCs are powered by the battery. A neat thing to remember is that most ESCs have internal 5V regulators, called **Battery Elimination Circuit** (**BEC**). This means we can power up Arduino from the ESC, by connecting the 5V output of the ESC to the 5V line on the Arduino.

Here's how it should look:

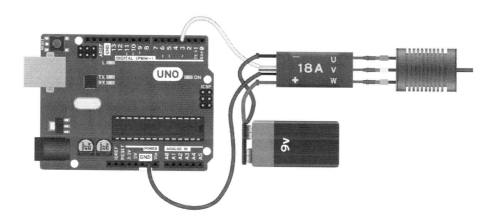

Code

The following code will arm the ESC and then start the motor for 5 seconds, stop it for another five, and do that again and again and again:

```
// Include the Servo library
#include <Servo.h>

// Declare the Servo pin for the ESC
int servoPin = 3;
// Create a servo object
Servo Servo1;

void setup() {
  // We need to attach the servo to the used pin number
  Servo1.attach(servoPin);
  // Arm the ESC, a pulse between 0.7 - 1 ms usually will do
  Servo1.writeMicroseconds(700);
  delay(3000); // Leave some time to arm the ESC
}

void loop(){
```

```
    // Start the motor a quarter speed
    Servo1.write(64);
    delay(5000); // Wait 5 seconds
    // Stop the motor for 5 seconds
    Servo1.write(0);
    delay(5000);
}
```

How it works...

Brushless motors and brushless motor control are quite advanced topics. Take a look at the *See also* section for more details on these. However, we don't really need to understand how they work in order to use them. That's what Arduino's all about: making things simple.

Brushless motor controllers or ESCs use the same standard as an RC servo. If we apply a pulse with a duration of 1 millisecond, or 0 degrees, in the `Servo.write()` function, the controller will stop the motor. A pulse of 2 milliseconds, or 180 degrees, will result in maximum power. Values in between will result in motor speeds in between.

Because brushless motors are quite powerful, every ESC has to be first armed in order to allow the motor to do anything. To do this, we send a pulse with a very low duration, somewhere between 0.7–1 millisecond for around 3 seconds. When the controller arms the motor, it will start buzzing a few times. After that, all the power can be unleashed.

Code breakdown

The code is very similar to the servo motor code, as both use the same standard. One difference is in the arming, as shown here:

```
void setup() {
  Servo1.attach(servoPin);
  // Arm the ESC
  Servo1.writeMicroseconds(700);
  delay(3000); // Leave some time to arm the ESC
}
```

We need to output a short pulse for around 3 seconds in order to arm the motor. We do this using the `Servo1.writeMicroseconds (700)` function, which outputs a 700-microsecond pulse.

Once the motor is armed, we can control it using standard `Servo1.write()` commands.

See also

▶   To understand how a brushless motor works, fined a great explanation in this video at `https://www.youtube.com/watch?v=bCEiOnuODac`

6
More Output Devices

In this chapter, we will cover the following topics:

- ▶ Creating sound
- ▶ Transistor driver
- ▶ Relay driver
- ▶ Optocouplers/Optoisolators
- ▶ More outputs – shift registers

Introduction

In this chapter, we will look over some more general applications of Arduino outputs. Sometimes, we don't have enough digital pins for our project, but we can extend that using shift registers! Also, we can try making some music by just adding a speaker. But what if we need to connect an AC circuit to the Arduino? All the answers, and more, can be found in this chapter.

Creating sound

Sound is a very powerful output that is usually taken for granted. We see things such as LEDs, we feel things such as motors, but we also hear. Arduino has a nice little library called Tone that aids in generating sounds at specific frequencies. For people passionate about music, we can actually play monophonic songs for the most geekish sound possible.

Getting ready

Following are the ingredients required to execute this recipe:

- ► An Arduino board connected to a computer via USB.
- ► A small 8-ohm speaker.
- ► A 120-ohm resistor; larger values also work, but the sound will be less powerful. Don't use resistors under 100 ohms.

How to do it...

Follow these steps to connect a speaker to the Arduino:

1. Connect one terminal of the speaker directly into the **GND** of the Arduino.
2. Using a 120-ohm resistor in series, connect the other terminal to an available digital pin; in this example, pin **12**.

Schematic

This is one possible implementation on the 13th digital pin. Other digital pins can also be used.

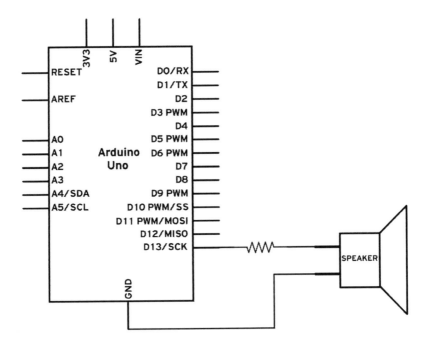

Here is an example of how to wire it in the air. No breadboard needed here:

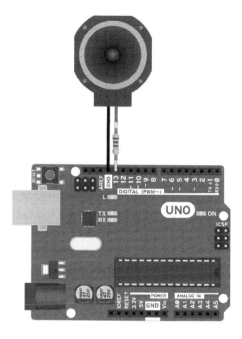

Code

The following code will play the famous Solfeggio—Do Re Mi Fa Sol La Ti:

```
// Defining the 8 frequencies that make the 7 notes and one
repetition in the Solfeggio
#define Do  131
#define Re  147
#define Mi  165
#define Fa  175
#define Sol 196
#define La  220
#define Ti  247
#define Do2 262

// Defining the pin connected to the speaker
int tonePin = 13;

void setup(){
```

```
                // Tone pins don't need to be declared
        }

        void loop(){
          // Do
          tone(tonePin, Do, 125);
          delay(125);
          // Re
          tone(tonePin, Re, 125);
          delay(125);
          // Mi
          tone(tonePin, Mi, 125);
          delay(125);
          // Fa
          tone(tonePin, Fa, 125);
          delay(125);
          // Sol
          tone(tonePin, Sol, 125);
          delay(125);
          // La
          tone(tonePin, La, 125);
          delay(125);
          // Ti
          tone(tonePin, Ti, 125);
          delay(125);
          // Higher Do
          tone(tonePin, Do2, 125);
          delay(125);
        }
```

 If the speaker is connected to a different pin, simply change the
tonePin value to the value of the pin that has been used.

How it works...

The tone() function is very easy to use. It generates a square wave of 50% duty cycle at the specified frequency. What does that mean? It means that the used pin will be HIGH half the time and LOW half the time. It will change between these two states at the specified frequency.

Every musical note has a specific frequency; in our case, Do, which is a C3, has the frequency of 131 Hz. This wave will make the speaker vibrate and generate sound. Arduino can only support monophonic sound using the Tone function. This means it can only generate one note at a time. Still, it is quite useful and fun. Now on to the code breakdown!

Code breakdown

The code simply uses the built-in tone function, which has the following parameters:

```
tone(pin, frequency, duration)
```

First, we declare the used pin:

```
int tonePin = 13;
```

Then, in `loop()`, we simply use the Tone function for each note, one after the other, with a duration of 125 milliseconds on the declared `tonePin`:

```
void loop(){
  // Do
  tone(tonePin, Do, 125);
  delay(125);
  ...
}
```

 We need to make sure we are not calling the `tone()` function again in the following 125 milliseconds, as it will change the frequency.

It would be easier to declare an array containing all the notes and use a `for` loop to play them all:

```
// Array approach
int solfege[] = {Do, Re, Mi, Fa, Sol, La, Ti, Do2};

for (int i = 0; i < 8; i++){
  tone(tonePin, solfege[i], 125);
  delay(125);
}
```

 The `tone()` function cannot play sounds under 31 Hz, and on boards other than the Mega, it will interfere with PWM pins 3 and 11.

There's more...

There is a little more functionality in the Tone function. Here are a few more things we can do:

- ▸ Tone with no duration
- ▸ Tone on multiple pins

Let's see what they are.

Tone with no duration

The `tone()` function has two variants. The one we used plays the note until the time expires or until we use the `tone()` function again, whichever comes first. However, there is a simpler variant that doesn't have the duration parameter; it only contains the pin and the frequency. When we use that function, the note will start playing continuously. In order to stop the note, we need to use the `noTone(tonepin)` function. Here is an example:

```
tone(tonePin, Do);
delay(100);
noTone(tonePin);
```

The `noTone()` function has only one parameter: the pin number. We need to use the same pin number as the one used in our `tone()` function; otherwise, it will not stop the sound and it might interfere with our code.

Tone on multiple pins

The Tone function can only play one note on one pin at a time. However, we can stop playing on a pin and begin playing on another one. In the following example, we play Do on the 12th pin and then Re on the 13th pin. This, of course, requires two speakers:

```
// Do on pin 12
tone(12, Do, 125);
delay(125);
noTone(12);

// Re on pin 13
tone(13, Re, 125);
delay(125);
noTone(13);
```

▸ For a reference for the frequencies of each note, visit `http://www.phy.mtu.edu/~suits/notefreqs.html`. Remember that Arduino cannot play frequencies under 31 Hz (C1 is the first note it can play). Wondering why it cannot play less than 31 Hz? Find out at `http://forum.arduino.cc/index.php?topic=28055.0`.

▸ If we want to use a more powerful speaker, we should amplify the limited power on the Arduino digital pins using a transistor driver. More details can be found in the *Transistor driver* recipe.

Transistor driver

Each Arduino digital pin can output a limited amount of current, an absolute maximum of 40 mA. This is enough to power an LED, a small *buzzer* speaker, or maybe a small vibrating motor. However, we need more current for our applications most of the time.

Using a transistor driver, we can easily power up more demanding loads. Here, we will quickly explore how to build a general transistor driver.

Getting ready

Following are the ingredients for this recipe:

▸ An Arduino board connected to a computer via USB

▸ A resistor between 220 and 4,700 ohm

▸ A standard NPN transistor (BC547, 2N3904, N2222A, TIP120)

▸ A standard diode (1N4148, 1N4001, 1N4007)

How to do it...

Follow these steps to connect an external load to the Arduino using an NPN transistor:

1. Connect one of the terminals of the load to **5V** or **VIN**. If we are using a load that requires a voltage higher than 5 V or higher current than the Arduino 5V can provide (around 500 mA), we can use the VIN pin and connect an external power supply or battery to the Arduino power connector.

2. Check the data sheet of the transistor. We need to correctly identify the base, collector, and emitter pins.

3. Connect the emitter pin to GND.

4. Connect the base pin of the transistor to one digital pin of the Arduino, using a resistor between 220 and 4,700 ohm.

5. Connect the other free terminal of the load to the collector.

6. For security reasons, connect a diode across the load resistor. The diode has to point from the collector to the power supply. This will protect the transistor from spikes generated by any inductive loads such as a motor or a relay.

Schematic

This is one possible implementation on the 9th digital pin. Other digital pins can also be used.

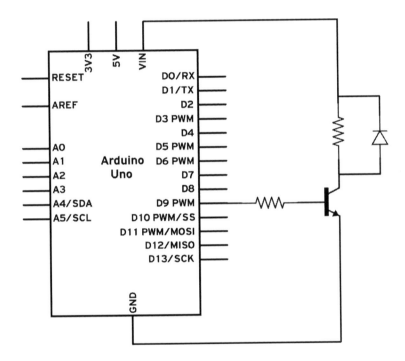

If the used load is polarized (it contains a positive and a negative terminal), connect the negative terminal to the collector on the NPN transistor and the positive terminal to the power supply that has been used (5V or VIN).

Code

The following code will turn the load on and off at an interval of 500 milliseconds:

```
// Declare the used pin
int loadPin = 9;

void setup(){
  // Declare the used pin as output
  pinMode(loadPin, OUTPUT);
}

void loop(){
  // Turn on the Load
  digitalWrite(loadPin, HIGH);
  delay(500);

  // 500 ms later, turn off the Load
  digitalWrite(loadPin, LOW);
  delay(500);
}
```

If the load is connected to a different pin, simply change the `loadPin` value to the value of the pin that has been used.

How it works...

When we set the digital pin as HIGH, using the `digitalWrite()` command, the transistor will get current in the base. When an NPN transistor receives enough current in the base, it will allow current to pass from the collector to the emitter, acting like a closed switch. When there is no current at the base, the collector and emitter pins will act like opened switches. This is a simple jelly-beam explanation of how a transistor works. The following graphic further explains the concept. A small current from the base to the emitter will allow a large current to pass from the collector to the emitter.

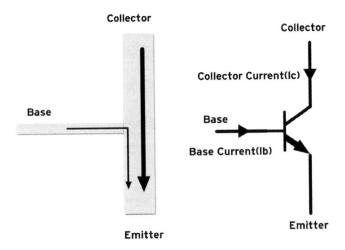

See also

This was a very simple introduction to how to use NPN transistors for general purposes. For more details, take a look at the following recipes:

- The *Controlling motors with transistors* recipe in *Chapter 5, Motor Control*
- The *Controlling speed with PWM* recipe in *Chapter 5, Motor Control*

Relay driver

Sometimes we just need to easily switch on and off an external load. Maybe the load is powered by AC current; maybe it's very high voltage that the Arduino can't handle. A transistor is usually used to power on such things; however, transistors are quite complicated. There is a simpler device that can just switch on or off, at slow speeds, an external load. This device is known as a relay.

Getting ready

To execute this recipe, we will need the following ingredients:

- An Arduino board connected to a computer via USB
- A general 5 V relay
- A resistor between 220 ohm and 4700 ohm
- A standard NPN transistor (BC547, 2N3904, N2222A, TIP120)
- A standard diode (1N4148, 1N4001, 1N4007)

How to do it...

The relay coil unfortunately uses quite a lot of current. To prevent this from burning the Arduino pins, we will use a transistor driver to start the relay:

1. Connect one of the terminals of the relay coil to the **5V** pin on the Arduino.
2. Check the data sheet of the transistor. We need to correctly identify the base, collector, and emitter pins.
3. Connect the emitter pin to **GND**.
4. Connect the base pin of the transistor to one digital pin of the Arduino using a resistor between 220 and 4,700 ohm.
5. Connect the other free terminal of the relay coil to the collector.
6. The relay is an inductive load. When we turn it off, it can create high voltage spikes that might burn the transistor. To protect against this, connect a diode from the collector to 5V, pointing to the 5V pin.

Schematic

This is one possible implementation. Other digital pins can also be used.

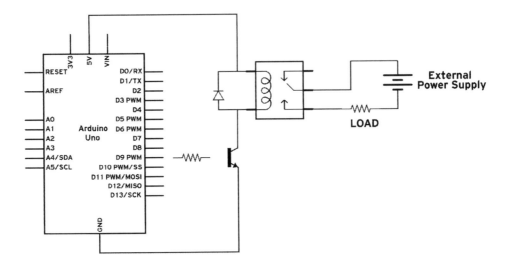

Code

In this recipe, we use the same code from the previous recipe, *Transistor driver*, which simply turns the relay on and off every 500 milliseconds:

```
// Declare the used pin
int relayPin = 9;

void setup(){
  // Declare the used pin as output
  pinMode(relayPin, OUTPUT);
}

void loop(){
  // Turn on the Relay
  digitalWrite(relayPin, HIGH);
  delay(3000);

  // 3 seconds later, turn off the Relay
  digitalWrite(relayPin, LOW);
  delay(3000);
}
```

If the transistor is connected to a different pin, simply change the `relayPin` value to the value of the pin that has been used.

How it works...

A relay is nothing more than a simple switch operated by current. When we apply enough current to the coil pins, it will generate an electromagnetic field that will close the switch. When we stop applying the current, the relay will release the switch back to the open position.

Each time we write a HIGH to the digital pin, the transistor switches the coil on and the internal switch in the relay closes. Now, electricity will pass between the two connected output terminals of the relay, and our load will receive current.

Relays are very good for switching AC currents. Also, the load circuit and the Arduino control circuits are completely independent, which is very safe. Another very important feature of any relay is that it can handle current in any direction; this is what makes it handle AC currents.

 This recipe uses a transistor driver in order to start the relay coil. For more details on how the transistor works, please check the *Transistor driver* recipe in this chapter.

Optocouplers/Optoisolators

There are times when we want to completely insulate two circuits, but still pass signals between them. We can do that with a relay. However, a relay is very slow. It takes around 10–30 milliseconds to switch on or off. We can't do PWM or communications at this pace. However, there is a clever **Integrated Circuit (IC)**, called either the optocoupler or the optoisolator, which does exactly that.

In this recipe, we will use an optocoupler to switch on an LED with a completely different circuit that has its own independent power supply.

Getting ready

Following are the ingredients needed for this recipe:

- An Arduino board connected to a computer via USB
- Two general 220-ohm to 1,000-ohm resistors
- A breadboard

▸ A 1.5–3.0 V battery, preferably with wire terminals

▸ A general LED

▸ A general optocoupler/optoisolator such as the TLP621, 4N35, or LTV-816

How to do it...

Following are the general steps to connect an optocoupler to the Arduino and then to connect another circuit containing an LED, resistor, and power supply to the optocoupler output:

1. Connect the anode (positive terminal of the LED) of the optocoupler to a digital pin on the Arduino, using a standard 220–1,000 ohm resistor.

2. Connect the cathode (LED negative terminal) of the optocoupler to **GND**.

3. Now the optocoupler is connected. We need to connect something to its output. In this case, we will connect an LED using a resistor and external power supply.

4. Connect the cathode of the LED (negative terminal) to the collector output on the optocoupler.

5. Connect the emitter output of the optocoupler to the negative terminal of the battery.

6. Use a standard 220–1,000 ohm resistor to connect the anode to the positive terminal of the battery.

Schematic

This is a typical implementation using digital pin 9:

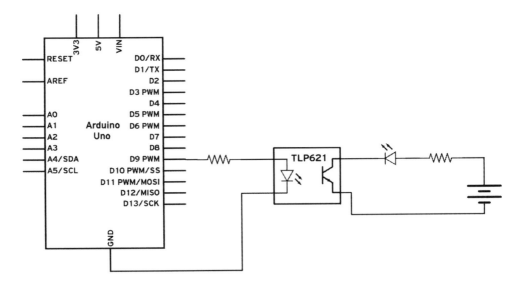

And on the breadboard, this works just fine:

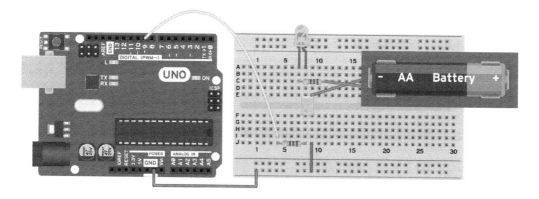

Code

We are using the same code from the previous recipe, *Transistor driver*, which simply turns the LED on and off using the optocoupler every 500 milliseconds:

```
// Declare the used pin
int optoPin = 9;

void setup(){
  // Declare the used pin as output
  pinMode(optoPin, OUTPUT);
}

void loop(){
  // Turn on the optocoupler
  digitalWrite(optoPin, HIGH);
  delay(500);

  // 500 ms later, turn off the optocoupler
  digitalWrite(optoPin, LOW);
  delay(500);
}
```

 If the optocoupler is connected to another digital pin, simply change the value of optoPin to the value of the digital pin that has been used.

How it works...

An optocoupler is made of an LED and a phototransistor. It is a clever little device. When we turn on the LED, it lights up the transistor. The difference between this phototransistor and a typical transistor is that the base is light-sensitive. When light hits it, it allows current to pass from the collector to the emitter. This makes the input and the output completely independent. Operation-wise, it works just like a transistor with an extra cathode pin for the LED input, which must be connected to the same ground as the Arduino.

More outputs – shift registers

Arduino has a limited number of digital pins. Sometimes, we want to build projects that require more pins than we have available on our boards. This is actually a common problem in electronics, which led to the invention of the shift register.

A shift register transforms serial data to parallel output. Basically, we tell the register what value to set for each output pin it has. If, for example, it has eight output pins, we will first say the value of the 8th pin and then the 7th pin until we get to the first one. The advantage is that we are using around three Arduino pins to get eight or even sixteen, which is very convenient.

There are a lot of shift registers available and they mostly work the same. For simplicity, we will only address the commonly available 74HC595 to control eight LEDs with just three pins.

Getting ready

For this recipe, we will require the following ingredients:

- An Arduino board connected to a computer via USB
- A 74HC595 shift register
- A breadboard along with jumper wires
- 8 LEDs
- 8 common resistors between 220–1,000 ohm

How to do it...

This is quite a big circuit, and putting it together requires some patience:

1. Plug in the 74HC595 in the center of the breadboard so that its pins go on each side. Be considerate with space; a lot will be used. It's better to mount it on one side of the breadboard.

2. Mount the eight LEDs and connect a 220–1,000 ohm series resistor to each.

3. Connect the cathode (negative terminal) of each LED to a common point and connect that point to the Arduino GND.

4. Connect the **GND** of the shift register to the Arduino GND. Also connect **VCC** and **MR** together to the Arduino 5V pin.

5. Connect each individual resistor to one of the output **Q0**, **Q1**, **Q2**, up to **Q7** pins.

Schematic

This is one possible implementation of the circuit. Other pins can be chosen to communicate with the shift register:

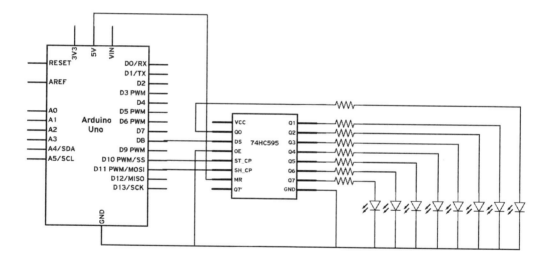

Here is an example of how to wire it on a breadboard:

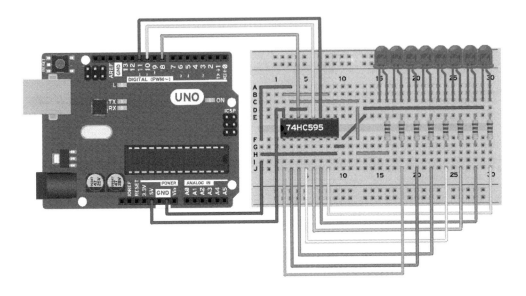

Code

The following code will make a flow illusion pattern on the LEDs:

```
// Declaring the 3 used pins to connect to the Register
int DS = 8;
int ST_CP = 10;
int SH_CP = 11;

// We make an Array with the values of each pin output on the
// Shift Register
boolean out[8];

void setup(){
  // Set the pins as outputs
  pinMode (DS, OUTPUT); // Pin for the actual data
  pinMode (ST_CP, OUTPUT); // Clock pin
  pinMode (SH_CP, OUTPUT); // Latch pin
}

void writePins(){
  // We first set the Latch Pin LOW
```

```
    digitalWrite(SH_CP, LOW);

    // Then we write each bit individually
    for(int i = 7; i>=0; i--){
      digitalWrite(ST_CP, LOW);
      digitalWrite(DS, out[i]);
      digitalWrite(ST_CP, HIGH);
    }

    // Latch the pin back
    digitalWrite(SH_CP, HIGH);
}

void loop(){
    // We will manually make each EVEN output HIGH
    out[0] = HIGH; out[1] = LOW;
    out[2] = HIGH; out[3] = LOW;
    out[4] = HIGH; out[5] = LOW;
    out[6] = HIGH; out[7] = LOW;
    // Write to the Shift Register
    writePins();
    delay (300);
    // And then each ODD output HIGH
    out[0] = LOW; out[1] = HIGH;
    out[2] = LOW; out[3] = HIGH;
    out[4] = LOW; out[5] = HIGH;
    out[6] = LOW; out[7] = HIGH;
    writePins();
    delay (300);
}
```

How it works...

The shift register has an input pin to which we send the values of the outputs. For example, on a shift register with four output pins—Q0, Q1, Q2, and Q3—if we send on the data pin in succession: 1,0,1,0, it will make Q0 high, Q1 low, Q2 high, and Q3 low.

However, we want to be able to write without affecting the current output of the shift register, and after we finish writing every output, we want to make the register apply the new values to its output pins. For this we use the latch pin. When we get the pin at LOW, in our case, it will not change the current output values until we put the pin at HIGH again. Also, it needs a way of knowing when we send a 1 or a 0; it needs a clock to make sure it reads each bit at the right interval. For that, we use the clock pin.

Code breakdown

First, we have to declare the three pins that have been used:

```
int DS = 8;
int ST_CP = 10;
int SH_CP = 11;
```

Then we make an array containing the output values LOW or HIGH of each shift register pin:

```
boolean out[8];
```

Now, we need to make a simple function that writes the values to the shift register. Inside it, we first latch the pin:

```
digitalWrite(SH_CP, LOW);
```

Following this, we need to give the clock to the register and input one bit at a time. We do this in a `for` loop. We need to go the opposite way in the array, as the register takes the values in reverse:

```
for(int i = 7; i>=0; i--){
    digitalWrite(ST_CP, LOW);
    digitalWrite(DS, out[i]);
    digitalWrite(ST_CP, HIGH);
}
```

At the end, we simply latch back the `SH_CP` pin:

```
digitalWrite(SH_CP, HIGH);
```

In `loop()`, we assign HIGH and LOW values to each output and then we use our `WritePins()` function to write those values:

```
out[0] = HIGH; out[1] = LOW;
out[2] = HIGH; out[3] = LOW;
out[4] = HIGH; out[5] = LOW;
out[6] = HIGH; out[7] = LOW;
// Write to the Shift Register
writePins();
```

7
Digital Communication with Arduino

In this chapter, we will cover the following recipes:

- ▸ Serial output
- ▸ Controlling the Arduino over serial
- ▸ Software serial and UART between Arduinos
- ▸ Wireless serial
- ▸ I2C between Arduinos
- ▸ SD cards
- ▸ LCD character displays
- ▸ Ethernet

Introduction

Arduino is not alone in the universe; it can use different digital communication protocols to talk with quite a few other systems. It's one of the great features of the platform; it has all of the standard protocols built in, allowing it to communicate with thousands of different devices.

Digital communication has numerous advantages. It is less susceptible to noise than analog communication, and it usually only requires two lines to communicate to hundreds of devices. This allows communication with the computer, with other microcontrollers such as the Arduino, with the Internet, and even pages to store data.

Serial output

This is the default for debugging and communication in the Arduino world. Whenever we want to determine what is happening in Arduino, how a sensor is performing or just general code debugging, we can use the serial output functions to write a message to the computer.

Here, we will explore the basics followed by a few tips and tricks on how to write different types of data. An important thing about serial communication on Arduino is that it can only be done between two devices. It is not possible to have three or more devices on the same serial connection.

Getting ready

Just one ingredient is needed for this recipe—an Arduino board connected to a computer via USB.

How to do it...

We just need to connect the Arduino to the computer and begin programming.

The following code will print half a Christmas tree in the serial monitor and then the values of two analog ports, providing the most common types of serial output encountered on Arduino:

```
void setup(){
  // Initialize the Serial communication with a 9600 baud rate
  Serial.begin(9600);
}

void loop(){
// Print a half Christmas tree
  for (int i = 1; i <= 8; i++){
    for ( int j = 0; j < i; j++){
      Serial.print("*");
    }
  Serial.println();
  }

  // Print the trunk of the half tree
  Serial.println("=");

  // Leave an empty space
```

```
    Serial.println("");

    // Read the value of A0 and print it
    int val = analogRead(A0);
    Serial.println (val);

    // Simpler way of printing a value
    Serial.println(analogRead(A1));

    // Leave an empty space
    Serial.println("");

    // A delay to not overflow the buffer and keep the terminal
    clean
    delay (500);
}
```

If everything works out, we should get the following output in the serial monitor:

```
*
**
***
****
*****
******
*******
********
=


299

296
```

How it works...

Whenever we want to write something to the computer, we use the built-in USB connection. However, the microcontroller inside the Arduino uses a UART connection, which is passed through a UART-USB converter. This creates the connection between the computer and Arduino. We will see how this works in the following subsection.

Code breakdown

The first thing we need to do is open a serial connection. We usually do this in the `setup()` function as we keep it open forever. The `Serial.begin(val)` function starts the connection. The `val` argument is the speed of the connection. Both devices need to be set to the same speed, which is called the baud rate. To set the rate on the PC side, use the box on the serial monitor window in Arduino.

In the `loop()` function, we first print the half Christmas tree. We use the `Serial.print("*")` function to print one asterisk character. When we finish a row, we create a new one using `println();`.

After this, we read a value from the analog port and print it on the serial port:

```
int val = analogRead(A0);
Serial.println (val);
```

We read the value of the `A0` port in the `val` variable and print it, going to a new line each time. In the next line, we use a more elegant way of printing out the value on the analog port `A1`:

```
Serial.println(analogRead(A1));
```

As a practice, try to make the full Christmas tree using for loops. Only then can you call yourself a master in the serial terminal.

See also

It is highly recommended to check the following recipes for proper motor control:

▶ The *Controlling the Arduino over serial* recipe

Controlling the Arduino over serial

In the *Serial output* recipe, we've seen how easy it is to print some data from Arduino to the computer. However, this can work the other way. In the serial monitor window in the Arduino IDE, we can write a string and send it to Arduino.

Here, you will learn what to do with that string and how you can use it to control things.

Getting ready

There is just one ingredient needed to implement this recipe—an Arduino board connected to a computer via USB.

How to do it...

Connect Arduino to the computer so that we can start programming it. The following code will start the built-in LED when it receives an `'a'`. It will stop the LED when it receives an `'x'`, and will blink it for a specified amount of time when it receives `'b'` followed by a number from 1 to 9, such as `'b4'`:

```
int led = 13;

void setup(){
  pinMode(led, OUTPUT);
  Serial.begin(9600);
}

void loop(){
  if (Serial.available()){
    char com = Serial.read();
    // Act according to the value received
    if (com == 'x'){
      // Stop the LED
      digitalWrite(led, LOW);
    }
    else if (com == 'a'){
      // Start the LED
      digitalWrite(led, HIGH);
    }
    else if (com == 'b'){
      // Blink with a delay corresponding to the value received
      after 'b'
      if (Serial.peek() > '0' && Serial.peek() <= '9'){
        digitalWrite(led, HIGH);
        delay((Serial.read() - 48) * 100); // 48 is ASCII for '0'
        digitalWrite(led, LOW);
      }
    }

  }
}
```

How it works...

Let's go through each section. First of all, we need to set up the LED pin as output and begin the serial connection with a baud rate of 9,600 bits per second:

```
void setup(){
  pinMode(led, OUTPUT);
  Serial.begin(9600);
}
```

In the `loop()` function, we want to receive the commands from the computer. Arduino has a serial buffer in which all received characters are stored. This is independent of the code we have running. First, let's check if there is anything in that buffer, otherwise there's no point in doing anything:

```
if (Serial.available()){
```

Now we need to read one character from the buffer. Each time we use the `Serial.read()` function, we erase the character from the buffer. So, the best thing will be to store it in a temporary variable. Since we are reading characters, we will use the char variable that only takes 8 bits of memory:

```
char com = Serial.read();
```

Everything gets simple from this point on; there are just a few things to remember. We can compare characters, all of them being part of the ASCII code. Take a look at the *See also* section of this recipe for a guide on ASCII. The following if clause will trigger when the received character is an `'x'` and will stop the LED:

```
if (com == 'x'){
  digitalWrite(led, LOW);
}
```

It's important to remember that, just like any other communication method, serial communication is susceptible to noise. This should always be taken into account when programming. Cascading `if` clauses is a good strategy. Whenever we design such an interpreter for the received characters, we should always make sure we only trigger for the characters we want; otherwise, some noise can corrupt things at any time.

Finally, we make the LED blink for a time equal to 100 milliseconds multiplied by the character received after 'b'. The `(Serial.read() - 48) * 100)` formula reads a character and subtracts 48. The `Serial.read()` function returns the ASCII equivalent, and in ASCII, 0 corresponds to 48, 1 corresponds to 49, and so on. Basically, this converts the character to a decimal value and then multiples it to 100.

We use the `Serial.peek()` function to read a character from the buffer without removing it. If we want to remove it, we use the `Serial.read()` function. Remember that Serial.peek() will always return the same character if no `Serial.read()` function is used.

There's more...

Serial communication is a huge subject in general. Here are a few more tips that should be useful.

Arduino Mega

There are a few Arduino platforms that have more than one serial/UART connection. In those cases, we won't be addressing using `Serial.read()`, `Serial.print()`, and so on. For them, we will be using `Serial1` instead of just `Serial`.

For example, `Serial1.begin(9600)` will start the first serial port with the baud rate of 9600. On an Arduino platform with multiple serial connections, `Serial1` is usually the one connected to the USB port. On the Arduino Yùn, however, we can use `Serial.begin()` for a USB connection.

Transmitting values to Arduino

There are times when we want to send a value from the computer to the Arduino. Let's design a small system that supports sending values from 0 to 999. In order to make everything simple, we will use a character that indicates that a number follows. The number will always have three characters. Thus, 0 will be represented by `'n000'` and 12 will be represented by `'n012'`. Here is the simple algorithm:

```
if (com == 'n'){
    int val = (Serial.read() - 48) * 100 +
              (Serial.read() - 48) * 10 +
              (Serial.read() - 48);
}
```

The first `Serial.read()` function will return the hundreds, the second one will return the tens, and the third one will return the unities.

See also

- You can find an ASCII table at `http://www.asciitable.com/`. This table is a very important concept for Arduino serial communication.

Software serial and UART between Arduinos

The serial port, professionally called **Universal Asynchronous Receiver/Transmitter** (**UART**) communication, is generally used to program and debug the Arduino via the USB port. There are multiple sensors and systems that use UART as the main communication method, and sometimes we need to discuss between two Arduinos to share information, workload, and so on.

However, most Arduinos only have one serial port, which is used by the USB connection. Serial communication can only happen between two devices. What can we do now? With a bit of luck, we'll have an Arduino Mega or similar that has up to four serial ports, but if we don't, there still is a solution. A special library has been written that simulates an UART port on other digital pins. There are a few drawbacks, but it generally works.

Getting ready

Following are the ingredients needed for this recipe:

▸ 2 Arduinos
▸ Jumper cables

How to do it...

Follow steps to connect two Arduino UNOs using software serial:

1. Assuming we use pins 8 and 9 for RX and TX on both Arduinos, connect pin 8 on one Arduino with pin 9 on the other one, and pin 9 on the first Arduino to pin 8 on the second one.
2. Connect the **GND** of both Arduinos together.
3. If we don't power up both Arduinos via USB, then we need to power up at least one and connect **5V** on each together.

Schematic

Here is an implementation using pins 8 and 9 for RX and TX:

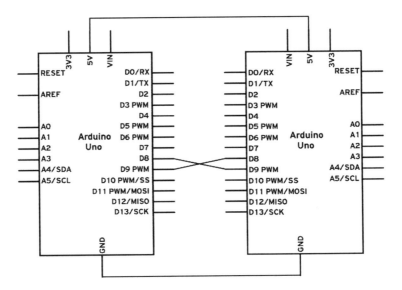

Here is a possible breadboard implementation:

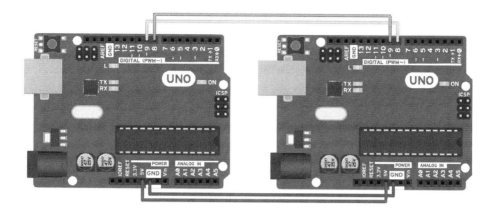

Code

The following code is split in two parts. The master Arduino will receive commands from the computer and write them over the soft serial. Take a look at the *Controlling the Arduino over serial* recipe in this chapter for more details about serial. Here's the first part of the code:

```
// Include the Software Serial library
#include <SoftwareSerial.h>

// Define a Software Serial object and the used pins
SoftwareSerial softSerial(8, 9); // RX, TX>

void setup(){
  Serial.begin(9600); // Normal Serial
  softSerial.begin(9600); // Soft Serial
}

void loop(){
  // Check for received characters from the computer
  if (Serial.available()){
    // Write what is received to the soft serial
    softSerial.write(Serial.read());
  }
}
```

And here is the slave code that interprets the characters sent from the master. If the character is `'a'`, it will start the built-in LED. If the character is `'x'`, it will stop it:

```
// Include the Software Serial library
#include <SoftwareSerial.h>

// Define a Software Serial object and the used pins
SoftwareSerial softSerial(8, 9); // RX, TX
// LED Pin
int LED = 13;

void setup(){
  softSerial.begin(9600); // Soft Serial
  pinMode(LED, OUTPUT); // Define LED pin mode
}

void loop(){
    // Check if there is anything in the soft Serial Buffer
  if (softSerial.available()){
    // Read one value from the soft serial buffer and store it in the
    variable com
    int com = softSerial.read();
    // Act according to the value received
    if (com == 'x'){
      // Stop the LED
      digitalWrite(LED, LOW);
    }
    else if (com == 'a'){
      // Start the LED
      digitalWrite(LED, HIGH);
    }
  }
}
```

How it works...

Software serial simulates a standard serial port on different digital pins on the Arduino. It is very handy in general; however, it is simulated, so it doesn't have dedicated hardware. This means it will take resources, particularly execution time and memory. Otherwise, it works just like a normal serial connection. All the functions present in the normal serial port are also present in software serial.

Code breakdown

First, we will look in the master, which takes characters received on the normal serial port and writes them to our simulated serial connection. In the beginning, we include the `SoftwareSerial.h` library:

```
#include <SoftwareSerial.h>
```

Then, we need to declare a serial object. We do so using the following syntax:

```
SoftwareSerial softSerial(8, 9); // RX, TX
```

The serial connection will be called, in this case, `softSerial`. It will use pin 8 for RX and pin 9 for TX. Take a look at the *There's more...* section for some information on which pins we can use.

Using the `softSerial` object, we can use all functions found in a normal serial connection, such as `softSerial.read()`, `softSerial.write()`, and so on. In this code, we check if there is anything in the real serial buffer. If there is, we read it from that buffer and we write it to the software serial:

```
if (Serial.available()){
    softSerial.write(Serial.read());
}
```

In the slave code, we run a simplified version of the code from the *Controlling the Arduino over serial* recipe, except that we use a software serial. This only changes the declaration and instead of writing `Serial.read()`, `Serial.available()`, and so on, we write `softSerial.read()` and `softSerial.available()`.

There's more...

Software serial has some important considerations and drawbacks. Here we tackle a few of them.

Usable pins

We can't use every pin on the Arduino for software serial. For TX, generally, anything can be used, but for the RX pin, only interrupt-enabled pins can. On the Arduino Leonardo and Micro, only pins 8, 9, 10, 11, 14, 15, and 16 can be used, while on the Mega or Mega 2560 only 10, 11, 12, 13, 50, 51, 52, 53, 62, 63, 64, 65, 66, 67, 68, and 69 can be used.

More software serial connections

It is possible to have more than one software serial connection; however, only one can receive data at a time. This will generally cause data loss. There is an alternative software serial library written by Paul Stoffregen, which tackles exactly this problem. The link can be found in the *See also* section of this recipe.

Interference

The software serial library uses the same timer as a few other libraries. This means that other functions might be affected by the use of a simulated serial port. The best known interference is with the Servo library. The best way to overcome this is to use the Arduino Mega, or something similar, which has four hardware serial ports—enough for any project.

General connection tips

UART connections are very simple; however, there are three key aspects to remember. Whenever connecting two serial devices, the TX pin on one device goes to the RX pin on the other device. If we do that the opposite way, we might kill the device! Also, the devices need to at least share the same **Ground** (**GND**). Lastly, the devices have to be set at the same speed, typically referred to as the baud rate.

See also

> ▸ Find an alternative to the software serial library written by Paul Stoffregen at
> `http://www.pjrc.com/teensy/td_libs_AltSoftSerial.html`

Wireless serial

Sometimes we just want to cut the wires and send data over air. Believe it or not, it's not that difficult. We can quickly transform a serial or software serial port into a wireless one if we have a wireless transmitter and receiver pair. These wireless components are quite cheap and easy to find. They are available in a few different frequencies, and they are very easy to set up.

We will use the code from the previous recipe, *Software serial and UART between Arduinos*; except that we will implement the serial over air. There is a catch; we can only send data in one direction.

Getting ready

To execute this recipe, we need the following ingredients:

> ▸ 2 Arduinos
>
> ▸ Jumper cables
>
> ▸ One RF link transmitter and RF link receiver pair

How to do it...

The following are the steps to connect two Arduino UNOs using Software Serial over wireless:

1. Assuming we use pins 8 and 9 for RX and TX on both Arduinos, connect pin 9 on the master Arduino to the **DATA** pin on the transmitter.

2. Connect pin 8 on the slave Arduino to the **DATA** pin of the receiver.

3. Connect the **GND** and the **5V** of the transmitter to the master Arduino.

4. Connect the **GND** and the **5V** of the receiver to the slave Arduino.

5. Use the same code as the previous recipe, *Software serial and UART between Arduinos*.

Schematic

Here is an implementation using pins 8 and 9 for RX and TX with the transmitter on the master Arduino and the receiver on the slave:

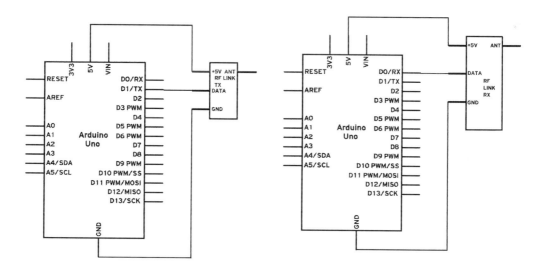

Here is a possible breadboard implementation:

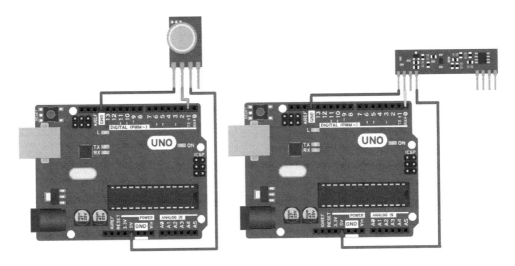

How it works...

The RF Link Transmitter Receiver pair is simple to set up and use. Basically, the transmitter outputs a radio signal corresponding to anything it gets on the DATA pin. In the same way, the receiver outputs anything it receives. They don't care about the baud rate as long as it is slow enough.

This kind of wireless communication is very susceptible to noise. It is recommended to use very low baud rates—9,600 or even 4,800 are good candidates. Also, the greater the distance, the more noise we get. In order to combat this we can, again, lower the baud rate.

There's more...

We can implement a two-way system if we use two RF Link pairs of different frequencies. If they are not of different frequencies, they will completely interfere with one another and both the master and the slave Arduinos will receive whatever is being transmitted by either.

See also

▸ There are, however, some professional modules designed to facilitate two-way serial communication. They are called Xbee and come in all kinds of flavors. More about these can be found at `https://www.sparkfun.com/pages/xbee_guide`.

I2C between Arduinos

Maybe sometimes we want to share the workload of one Arduino with another. Or maybe we want more digital or analog pins. **Inter-Integrated Circuit** or **I2C** (pronounced I squared C) is the best solution.

I2C is an interesting protocol. It's usually used to communicate between components on motherboards in cameras and in any embedded electronic system.

Here, we will make an I2C bus using two Arduinos. We will program one master Arduino to command the other slave Arduino to blink its built-in LED once or twice depending on the received value.

Getting ready

Following are the ingredients needed for this recipe:

▸ 2 Arduinos

▸ Jumper cables

How to do it...

Follow these steps to connect two Arduino UNOs using I2C:

1. Connect pins **A4** and **A5** on one Arduino to the same pins on the other one.
2. The **GND** line has to be common for both Arduinos. Connect it with a jumper.

Schematic

Here is a simple implementation. There is no need for a breadboard.

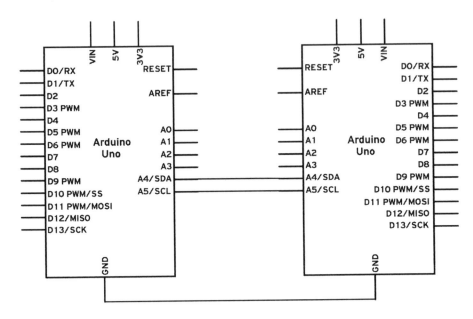

Here is a possible breadboard implementation:

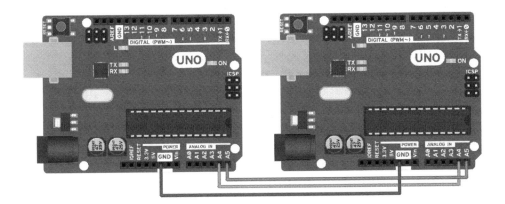

Remember never to connect 5 V and 3.3 V Arduinos together. It won't hurt the 5V Arduino, but it will certainly annoy its 3.3 V brother.

Code

The following code is split in two parts: the master code and the slave code, which run on two different Arduinos. First, let's take a look at the master code:

```
// Include the standard Wire library for I2C
#include <Wire.h>

int x = 0;

void setup() {
  // Start the I2C Bus as Master
  Wire.begin();
}

void loop() {
  Wire.beginTransmission(9);  // transmit to device #9
  Wire.write(x);              // sends x
  Wire.endTransmission();     // stop transmitting

  x++; // Increment x
  if (x > 5) x = 0; // reset x once it gets 6

  delay(500);
}
```

And here is the slave code that interprets the characters sent from the master:

```
#include <Wire.h>

int LED = 13;
int x = 0;

void setup() {
  pinMode (LED, OUTPUT);
  // Start the I2C Bus as Slave on address 9
  Wire.begin(9);
  // Attach a function to trigger when something is received.
```

```
    Wire.onReceive(receiveEvent);
}

void receiveEvent(int bytes) {
  x = Wire.read();      // read one character from the I2C
}

void loop() {
  //If value received is 0 blink LED for 200 ms
  if (x == '0') {
    digitalWrite(LED, HIGH);
    delay(200);
    digitalWrite(LED, LOW);
    delay(200);
  }
  //If value received is 3 blink LED for 400 ms
  if (x == '3') {
    digitalWrite(LED, HIGH);
    delay(400);
    digitalWrite(LED, LOW);
    delay(400);
  }
}
```

How it works...

To briefly go through the theory, I2C requires two digital lines: **Serial Data line (SDA)** to transfer data and **Serial Clock Line (SCL)** to keep the clock. Each I2C connection can have one master and multiple slaves. A master can write to slaves and request the slaves to give data, but no slave can directly write to the master or to another slave. Every slave has a unique address on the bus, and the master needs to know the addresses of each slave it wants to access. Now let's go through the code.

Code breakdown

First, let's look at the master. We need to include the required `Wire.h` library:

```
#include <Wire.h>
```

Then, in the setup function, we begin the I2C bus using the `Wire.begin()` function. If no argument is provided in the function, Arduino will start as a master.

Lastly, we send a character x, which is between 0 and 5. We use the following functions to begin a transmission to the device with the address 9, write the character, and then stop the transmission:

```
Wire.beginTransmission(9);   // transmit to device #9
Wire.write(x);               // sends x
Wire.endTransmission();      // stop transmitting
```

Now let's explore the slave Arduino code. We also include the `Wire.h` library here, but now we start the I2C bus using `Wire.begin(9)`. The number in the argument is the address we want to use for the Arduino. All devices with address 9 will receive the transmission.

Now we need to react somehow when we receive an I2C transmission. The following function appends a trigger function whenever a character is received. Better said, whenever the Arduino receives a character on I2C, it will run the function we tell it to run:

```
Wire.onReceive(receiveEvent);
```

And this is the function. Here, we simply store the value of the received character:

```
void receiveEvent(int bytes) {
    x = Wire.read();
}
```

In `loop()`, we simply interpret that character to blink the built-in LED at different speeds depending on the received character.

There's more...

I2C is a complicated transmission protocol, but it's very useful. All Arduinos implement it, with a few differences in pin mappings.

Comparing different Arduino categories

The pins for I2C are different in different Arduino categories. Here are the most common:

Board	I2C pins
Uno, Pro Mini	A4 (SDA), A5 (SCL)
Mega, Due	20 (SDA), 21 (SCL)
Leonardo, Yún	2 (SDA), 3 (SCL)

More about I2C

Each I2C bus can support up to 112 devices. All devices need to share GND. The speed is around 100 kb/s—not very fast but still respectable and quite useable. It is possible to have more than one master on a bus, but it's really complicated and generally avoided.

A lot of sensors use I2C to communicate, typically Inertial Measurement Units, barometers, temperature sensors, and some Sonars. Remember that I2C is not designed for long cable lengths. Depending on the cable type used, 2 m might already cause problems.

Connecting more devices

If we need to connect more than two devices on an I2C bus, we just have to connect all SDA and SCL lines together. We will need the address of every slave to be addressed from the master Arduino.

See also

> ▶ You can find a good explanation on how a master should request information to a slave at `http://arduino.cc/en/Tutorial/MasterReader`. This is an example closer to real life, as this is the way we usually request information from sensors.

SD cards

SD cards are great to store data in the long term. Arduino has a library specifically designed to talk to them. With this library, we can create, write, read, and destroy files. This is very handy, especially in data logging applications. We can have an Arduino running for months, recording data, and writing it to the SD card.

In this example, we will read the data from two analog ports and write it to the SD card.

Getting ready

The following are the ingredients needed for this recipe:

> ▶ An Arduino board connected to a computer via USB.
>
> ▶ A formatted SD card; Arduino accepts only FAT16 or FAT32 formatting.
>
> ▶ An Ethernet shield or any other Arduino-compatible SD shield.
>
> ▶ Optionally, two analog sensors. We will store their values on the SD card. It works without them, but we will only record random values on the analog ports.

How to do it...

Follow these steps to prepare to use an SD card:

1. Plug the Arduino-compatible SD shield into the Arduino.
2. Format the SD card to either FAT16 or FAT32.
3. Insert the SD card into the SD card slot on the shield.

Code

The following code will read the analog values from A0 and A1 and write them to the log.txt file on the SD card:

```
#include <SD.h>

// Declare the selectSPI pin. Pin 4 for the Ethernet shield
int selectSPI = 4;

void setup(){
  Serial.begin(9600); // Serial for debugging
  // Declare the standard selectSPI pin as OUPTUT. Pin 53 for Mega-
  like boards
  pinMode(10, OUTPUT);
  // Check if there is any SD card present
  if (!SD.begin(selectSPI)) {
    Serial.println("Card not found");
    return; // stop execution
  }
  Serial.println("Card found");
}

void loop(){
  // Read A0 and A1
   int val1 = analogRead(A0);
   int val2 = analogRead(A1);

  // Open the file
  File logFile = SD.open("log.txt", FILE_WRITE);
  // Check if the file is available
  if (logFile) {
    logFile.print(val1); // Write first value
    logFile.print(" "); // Write a space
    logFile.println(val2); // Write second value
    logFile.close(); // close the file
  } else {
    // if the file can't be opened, alert
    Serial.println("error opening file");
  }
}
```

How it works...

SD cards use a technology called **Serial Protocol Interface** (**SPI**) to communicate. Arduino has one SPI connection embedded into it. In the code breakdown, we will explore how it all works.

Code breakdown

The first thing we do is include the SD.h library. After that, we initialize a variable that will represent the select pin for SPI. SPI can handle communication between multiple devices. In order to know which device we are addressing, a select pin is implemented. In the case of the Ethernet shield, which embeds an SD card adapter, this is pin number 4.

Following this, and due to the way SPI is implemented in the Arduino microcontroller, we need to select the standard select pin as Output, regardless of whether we are using it. For standard Arduinos, that is pin 10 and for Mega, it's pin 53:

```
pinMode(10, OUTPUT);
```

Now we can start the connection and check if any card is present. If not, we will stop the program completely. We need to tell the SD library the select pin on which it can find the SD card:

```
if (!SD.begin(selectSPI)) {
    Serial.println("Card not found");
    return; // stop execution
}
```

In the `loop()` function, we read the value of the two analog ports. After that, we open the file using the following function:

```
File logFile = SD.open("log.txt", FILE_WRITE);
```

If the file doesn't exist, it will be created. We should check if the file is available for writing. We use an `if` clause on the logFile file. If it is available, we will simply write to it:

```
if (logFile) {
    logFile.print(val1); // Write first value
    logFile.print(" "); // Write a space
    logFile.println(val2); // Write second value
    logFile.close(); // close the file
}
```

Otherwise, we just alert using the serial connection that we started for debugging.

There's more...

SD cards and SPIs are quite complex in general. Here are a few things to know:

- **Not all cards work**: There are cases when fast cards will not work. Generally, cards of class 4 work well, while cards of class 6 and faster present problems. To easily find information about a card, run the Arduino IDE built-in example found under **File | Examples | SD | CardInfo**. It will print out all the details it can acquire about the SD card.

- **Reading from SD cards**: Reading is of course possible. It uses the same protocol as the serial connection. The Arduino IDE example ReadWrite found under **File | Examples | SD** gives a good explanation.

- **Note on electronic connections**: Most Arduinos work on 5 V while the standard for SD cards is 3.3 V. The Ethernet shield and other Arduino-compatible SD shields all have a built-in logic level shifter that shifts the voltages from 5 V to 3.3 V and vice versa. If we are implementing a custom SD card connector, we should at least use a voltage divider for the output signals from the Arduino to the SD; otherwise, we will burn the SD card. Sparkfun sells a very handy Logic Level Shifter, which will work perfectly in this application.

LCD character displays

There is nothing better than writing any information from the Arduino to a small LCD character display. They are incredibly handy and just look plain cool. Even better, Arduino has a built-in library to do this. Let's explore how we can implement it.

Getting ready

We will need the following ingredients for this recipe:

- An Arduino board connected to a computer via USB
- An LCD character display of any dimension—16 x 2 is the standard size
- A 10K-ohm potentiometer
- Jumper wires

How to do it...

First, we need to connect the monitor to the Arduino. This generally requires a minimum of 6 digital pins as shown in the following diagram:

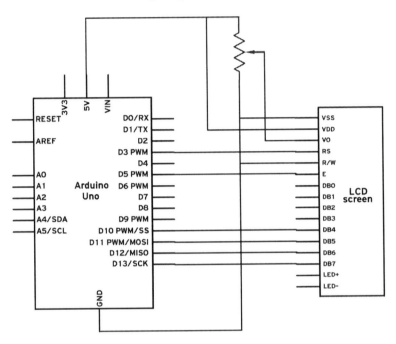

This is one possible breadboard implementation:

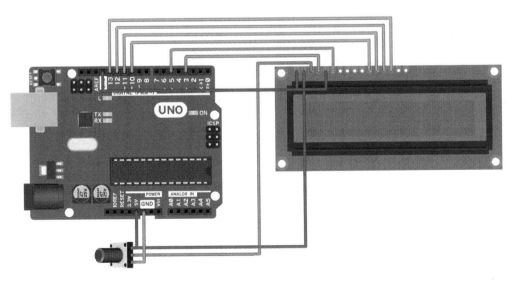

Follow these steps to connect an LCD to the Arduino:

1. Connect **GND** to the **VSS** and **R/W** pins.

2. Connect **5V** to the **Vcc/Vdd** input.

3. Connect 6 digital pins to **E** (enable), **RS**, and **DB4**-**DB7**. This is the 4-bit way of connecting HD44780-based displays, such as the common LCD character displays.

4. Lastly, connect a 10K-potentiometer with the central, moving tap to pin **Vo**, one pin to **5V**, and one to **GND**. By adjusting this potentiometer, we are adjusting the contrast of the display.

Code

The following code will print `"Hello Arduino"` on the first line, and on the second line it will print the number of seconds passed:

```
// Include the required LCD library
#include <LiquidCrystal.h>

// Initialize a LCD and pass the pins in the order rs, enable, d4,
d5, d6, d7
LiquidCrystal lcd(3, 5, 10, 11, 12, 13);

void setup(){
  // Begin the LCD with the number of columns and rows
  lcd.begin(16, 2);
}

void loop(){
    // Set cursor at beginning column and row:
    lcd.setCursor(0, 0); // lcd.home() does the same
    lcd.print ("Hello Arduino!");
    // Set cursor at beginning of second row
    lcd.setCursor(0, 1);
    lcd.print (millis()/1000);
}
```

 Any digital pins can be used to connect an LCD as long as they are not used by anything else.

How it works...

Almost all LCD character displays use the Hitachi HD44780 driver standard, which is implemented as a library in the Arduino environment. Each LCD has a number of columns and rows, with the most typical configurations being 8 x 2, 16 x 2, and 20 x 4. We require at least six digital pins to control these displays.

Code breakdown

Initially, we just include the `LiquidCrystal.h` library. Then we create a Liquid Crystal object called `LCD` in which we write the pin numbers used:

```
LiquidCrystal lcd(3, 5, 10, 11, 12, 13);
```

Afterwards, in the `setup()` function, we initialize the display using `lcd.begin(columns, rows)`. In the end, we can simply jump to any location and write anything we want:

```
lcd.setCursor(0, 0);
lcd.print ("Hello Arduino!");
lcd.setCursor(0, 1);
lcd.print (millis()/1000);
```

There's more...

There are a few more things we can do with LCDs:

▶ **More ways of connecting**: In this example, we implemented the simplest of all versions. It requires the minimum amount of cables; however, there are four types in total:

   ❑ `LiquidCrystal(rs, enable, d4, d5, d6, d7)`
   ❑ `LiquidCrystal(rs, rw, enable, d4, d5, d6, d7)`
   ❑ `LiquidCrystal(rs, enable, d0, d1, d2, d3, d4, d5, d6, d7)`
   ❑ `LiquidCrystal(rs, rw, enable, d0, d1, d2, d3, d4, d5, d6, d7)`

Having access to the RW pin will allow us to read from the monitor, which is not really useful as we are the ones who also write on it. Usually, this pin is just connected to GND to make it stay in receive mode. Using all eight data lines is not necessary but is twice as fast as only using four.

There are also some I2C-based LCD displays that only require the two I2C pins. If we are tight on pins, that is the solution.

▸ **No image**: When we set up the circuit for the first time, there are a lot of chances of no text showing up. We should play with the contrast potentiometer to make sure it's not killing or supersaturating the contrast.

▸ **Backlight**: Some LCD displays also have a built-in backlight. Check the datasheet for the screen used to find out how to enable it. Most require an external resistor that is always specified in the datasheet.

Ethernet

Using an Ethernet shield, we can connect an Arduino to the Internet. All the power and awesomeness of the Internet can come to this small blue board we are programming. This is a huge topic; however, the Arduino Ethernet library makes it all simple.

Here, we will create an interesting application for this functionality. We will make the Arduino a local web server to which we can connect to find out the readings of the first three analog inputs, using our browser.

Getting ready

The following are the ingredients needed for this recipe:

▸ An Arduino

▸ An Arduino Ethernet shield

▸ A router or just an Ethernet cable

How to do it...

Follow these steps to build the server:

1. Carefully plug the Ethernet shield into the Arduino.
2. Connect an Ethernet cable to the shield.
3. Connect the other end of the Ethernet cable to the same router to which your computer is connected.

Code

The following code attempts to connect to a router using DHCP. Once it does, it will output the IP via serial and then it will wait for incoming connections. When a connection is set, it will output the values of the first three analog inputs via an HTML page. The code is as follows:

```
// Include the required SPI and Ethernet Libraries
#include <SPI.h>
```

```
#include <Ethernet.h>

// MAC Address for the Ethernet Shield
byte mac[] = {0x00, 0xAA, 0xBB, 0xCC, 0xDD, 0x01};

// Create an Ethernet Server object on port 80
EthernetServer server(80);

void setup() {
  Serial.begin(9600); // Start Serial

  // Start the Ethernet connection and check if succeeded
  while (Ethernet.begin(mac) == 0) {
    Serial.println("Failed to configure Ethernet using DHCP");
    delay(500);
  }

  Serial.println("Connection Established");

  // Print the IP Address
  Serial.print("Server IP address: ");
  Serial.println(Ethernet.localIP());
}

void loop() {
  // Check for clients
  EthernetClient client = server.available();

  // When there is a client
  if (client) {
    while (client.connected()) {
      if (client.available()) {

        // GET requests from clients end in an empty newline
        // If a newline character is found and the second
        character is a newline
        if (client.read() == '/n' && client.read() == '/n') {
          // Send a HTTP response

          // HTTP header:
          client.println("HTTP/1.1 200 OK");
          client.println("Content-Type: text/html");
          client.println("Connection: close");  // Connection
          closes after response
```

```
    client.println("Refresh: 3");   // Refresh page every 3
    seconds
    client.println();

    // HTML Page:
    client.println("<!DOCTYPE HTML>");
    client.println("<html> <body>");

    // Write the values of the first 3 Analog Inputs in
    paragraphs
    for (int anIn = 0; anIn < 3; anIn++) {
      client.print("<p>"); // Begin paragraph
      client.print("Analog Input ");
      client.print(anIn); // Print the analog input number
      client.print(" = ");
      client.print(analogRead(anIn)); // Print channel value
      client.println("</p>"); // End paragraph
    }

    client.println("</body> </html>");
      }
    }
  }
}
  // Allow message to be processed by browser
  delay(10);
  // Close connection to client
  client.stop();
  Serial.println("Client Disconnected");
  }
}
```

How to test

If the Ethernet shield is plugged in to the same router as your computer, check for the IP the Arduino gives over serial. Then, in your browser address bar, write that IP and hit *Enter*. It will take you to the custom page.

How it works...

The Ethernet shield has a powerful processor inside, designed just to tackle all the protocols of Ethernet, TCP, UDP, and so on. It is a very advanced component. The shield uses the SPI communication protocol for high-speed communication with the Arduino. Thankfully, Arduino has a library to simplify everything, as we can see in the code breakdown.

Code breakdown

Both SPI and Ethernet libraries have to be included for this bad boy to work:

```
#include <SPI.h>
#include <Ethernet.h>
```

Anything connected to the Internet or any local network requires a unique MAC address. Here, we will write a random one in a byte array and hope no other device has it:

```
byte mac[] = {0x00, 0xAA, 0xBB, 0xCC, 0xDD, 0x01};
```

We need to create an `EthernetServer` object to tackle all the complex connection protocols. The argument of the function is the port on which the server will listen for connections. Port 80 is the standard:

```
EthernetServer server(80);
```

Here, we attempt to start the Ethernet connection with the specified MAC address. If it fails and returns 0, it will attempt again. However, there are few chances if it doesn't work from the first attempt. This is the required code:

```
while (Ethernet.begin(mac) == 0) {
    Serial.println("Failed to configure Ethernet using DHCP");
    delay (500);
}
```

Once the DHCP has been set, we need to know the IP of the server. The following function will print the IP address over the serial:

```
Serial.print("Server IP address: ");
Serial.println(Ethernet.localIP());
```

In the `loop()` function, we first declare a variable of type `EthernetClient`, which will take the value of the availability of a client:

```
EthernetClient client = server.available();
```

Once we have a client, while it is connected, we check if it is available, using the following syntax:

```
if (client) {
    while (client.connected()) {
        if (client.available()) {
```

Now we need to listen to GET commands from the client. These commands request information to be sent back to the client. At the end of each GET request, we have an empty line that we can find using the following syntax:

```
if (client.read() == '/n' && client.read() == '/n') {
```

If we detect such a command, we respond with a website. Each website starts with a HTTP answer header, which includes some basic details about the connection and the website. In our case, we tell the browser to refresh every three seconds to see the updates in the values:

```
client.println("HTTP/1.1 200 OK");
        client.println("Content-Type: text/html");
        client.println("Connection: close");
        client.println("Refresh: 3");
        client.println();
```

And then we write the actual website HTML code. For more details about HTML, take a look at the *See also* section of this recipe.

In the end, we close the connection and loop back to wait for other connections.

There's more...

We can actually make this data available across the Internet, but for this we need to have a private IP address. If indeed we have one of these, we can change the connection code to the following:

```
byte mac[] = {0xDE, 0xAD, 0xBE, 0xEF, 0xFE, 0xED};
IPAddress ip(192, 168, 1, 177); // Your private IP
EthernetServer server(80);
```

This will set up the server using the specified IP. If indeed we have a private IP and we start the server on that IP, we can access it from anywhere in the world by just typing that IP address into our browser address bar.

See also

- ▶ The Ethernet shield can do a ton of things. For more information about it, visit http://arduino.cc/en/Reference/Ethernet.

- ▶ For an HTML primer, visit http://www.w3schools.com/html/.

8
Hacking

In this chapter, we will cover the following topics:

- ▸ More digital pins
- ▸ Faster PWM
- ▸ Storing data internally – EEPROM
- ▸ Timing Arduino code
- ▸ External interrupts

Introduction

This chapter is for the rebels! It's about the tips and tricks that push the Arduinos development a little to the edge. Sometimes, we may want to execute some code at precisely the time something happens, even when we are doing something completely different. Or we may want to store data within Arduino even if we power it off. All of that and more can be learned in this chapter, folks!

More digital pins

There are times when we need more digital pins on the Arduino without any other external components. An Arduino Uno has 14 digital pins, from 0 to 14, right? Wrong! It actually has 20. The analog in ports can at all times be used as digital ports, and they have all the functionality of normal digital ports.

A word of caution: pins 0 and 1 are the UART ports used for programming need to take extra care about what we connect there, because when we are programming the board, those pins will switch from HIGH to LOW thousands of times.

Getting ready

Just one ingredient is needed for this recipe—an Arduino Board connected to a computer via USB.

How to do it...

The following code shows how to use pins A0 and A1 as normal digital pins:

```
void setup(){
  pinMode(A0, OUTPUT);
  pinMode(A1, OUTPUT);
}

void loop(){
  digitalWrite(A0, HIGH);
  digitalWrite(A1, LOW);
  delay(500);

  digitalWrite(A0, LOW);
  digitalWrite(A1, HIGH);
  delay(500);
}
```

How it works...

Internally, all pins on Arduino boards have different functions. The only function they all share is the basic digital input and output. All of them can output either HIGH or LOW and all of them can read either HIGH or LOW.

In other words, all of the following functions will work the same way as on any random digital port:

```
pinMode(A0, OUTPUT);
pinMode(A1, INPUT);
pinMode(A2, INPUT_PULLUP); // Set as an input with PULL UP
resistor
digitalWrite(A0, LOW);
digitalRead(A1);
```

Faster PWM

This is an exotic procedure! The standard PWM frequency on the Arduino is around 490 Hz. While it can get most jobs done, it is not really that fast. However, we can change that.

Faster PWM is especially useful when controlling motors. At low PWM, the torque is greatly affected, and it can also create audible noise. The best way to test this is to implement the *Controlling speed with PWM* recipe from *Chapter 5, Motor Control*, and increase the PWM frequency.

> A note to remember: this might interfere with other functions, such as `delay()`. We have to be extra careful when this happens.

Getting ready

Following are the ingredients required to implement this recipe:

- An Arduino board connected to a computer via USB
- A DC motor
- A resistor between 220 ohm and 4,700 ohm
- A standard NPN transistor (BC547, 2N3904, N2222A, TIP120) or a logic level-compatible MOSFET (IRF510, IRF520)
- A standard diode (1N4148, 1N4001, 1N4007)

How to do it...

After we implement the same circuit as in the *Controlling speed with PWM* recipe from *Chapter 5, Motor Control*, which starts a motor on pin 9, we just have to add one line to the `setup()` function:

```
// Declare the pin for the motor
int motorPin = 9;

void setup() {
  // Change Timer 1 divider which will make the PWM faster
  // In this Setting it will have a frequency of 31372.55 Hz
  TCCR1B = TCCR1B & 0b11111000 | 0x01;
}

void loop(){
  // Fade the motor in
```

```
for (int i = 0; i < 256; i ++){
  analogWrite(motorPin, i);
  delay(20);
}
// Stop the motor
analogWrite(motorPin, 0);
delay(2000);
}
```

How it works...

Internal timers inside the ATMega chip drive PWM pins on each Arduino. A timer is a component that keeps time; shocking, isn't it? The Arduino UNO has three such timers:

- Timer 0
- Timer 1
- Timer 2

Two PWM pins are assigned to each of these timers. Pins 9 and 10 are assigned to Timer 1, pins 11 and 3 to timer 2, and pins 5 and 6 to Timer 0. Timers 1 and 2 share the same PWM frequency of 490 Hz while Timer 0 is the rebel with a whopping 976 Hz.

Each timer has an internal prescaler that divides the clock rate, which is typically given by the 16 MHz quartz oscillator. If we change the prescaler value, all functions allocated to that timer will change the frequency. PWM is one of those functions. There is just one line of code that changes the divider of one timer:

```
TCCR1B = TCCR1B & 0b11111000 | 0x01;
```

Now that looks funky. It actually is very simple. All we need to know is that TCCRxB represents timer x. So timer 0 is TCCR0B, timer 1 is TCCR1B, and so on. The full syntax is as follows:

```
TCCRxB = TCCRxB & 0b11111000 | setting;
```

Here x is the timer number and setting is the setting we are using to change the divider. The following tables will elucidate everything.

Timer 0

This timer controls the PWM pins 5 and 6. Please read the *There's more...* section of this recipe about interference with the delay() function.

Setting	Divider	Frequency
0x01	1	62,500 Hz
0x02	8	7,812.5 Hz

Setting	Divider	Frequency
0x03	64	976.5625 Hz (Default)
0x04	256	244.14 Hz
0x05	1024	61.035 Hz

So if we want to make Timer 0 run at 62500 Hz, we have to implement in the setup() function:

```
TCCR0B = TCCR0B & 0b11111000 | 0x01;
```

Timer 1

This is responsible for PWM pins 9 and 10.

Setting	Divider	Frequency
0x01	1	31,372.55 Hz
0x02	8	3,921.16 Hz
0x03	64	490.20 Hz (Default)
0x04	256	122.55 Hz
0x05	1024	30.64 Hz

Timer 2

This is responsible for PWM pins 11 and 3.

Setting	Divider	Frequency
0x01	1	31,372.55 Hz
0x02	8	3,921.16 Hz
0x03	32	980.39 Hz
0x04	64	490.20 Hz (Default)
0x05	128	245.10 Hz
0x06	256	122.55 Hz
0x07	1024	30.64 Hz

We can modify the setting of all three timers if we want, by writing the three modifiers in the setup() function.

All of this can be found under the *Timer/Counter0 and Timer/Counter1 Prescalers* section in the ATmega328P datasheet. Take a look at the *See also* section of this recipe.

There's more...

There are a few more things to know about this exotic procedure.

Interference

Timers are very important in the Arduino world. A lot of functions and libraries use them. When we change the frequency of the timer, it affects the frequency of all libraries that use it. The `Servo`, `Stepper`, `SoftwareSerial`, or even basic functions such as `delay()` will be affected. Here we will talk about the `delay()` function.

The `delay()` function uses Timer 0 to record the time passed. If we change the divider on the timer, it will directly affect the function. For example, if we change the setting from the default 0x03 to 0x02, it will change the divider from 64 to 8; we will thus make the function eight times faster. This means that `delay(1000)` will not last 1,000 milliseconds but 125 milliseconds. To correct this, we can now write `delay(8000)`, which will run for a full second.

Pay great attention to the functionality the timer division change affects. Even common everyday things can be affected. The best way to find out is through experimentation. If something no longer works after a timer division change, you have the culprit.

Other Arduinos

All Arduinos have internal timers. In order to change them, we have to check the datasheet of the ATMega inside the used Arduino and see what settings we can change. For example, the Arduino Mega and Mega 2560 have the following timers linked to the following pins:

Timer	PWM pins
Timer 0	4, 13
Timer 1	11, 12
Timer 2	9, 10
Timer 3	2, 3, 5
Timer 4	6, 7, 8

See also

- For more information about Timer and PWM hacking, read this article by Ken Shirriff at `http://arduino.cc/en/Tutorial/SecretsOfArduinoPWM`.
- A better way to have more control over PWM is to use specialized ICs that do just that. Here is a very nice PWM Shield from Sparkfun, which you can find at `https://www.sparkfun.com/products/10615`.

▸ The biblical datasheet of the ATMega328P, the brain of the Arduino Uno can be found at `http://www.atmel.com/images/Atmel-8271-8-bit-AVR-Microcontroller-ATmega48A-48PA-88A-88PA-168A-168PA-328-328P_datasheet_Complete.pdf`.

Storing data internally – EEPROM

Sometimes we want to store some values inside the Arduino even when we turn it off. Luckily, each Arduino has an internal **Electrically Erasable Programmable Read-Only Memory** (**EEPROM**) just for that.

A note for using EEPROM-–the EEPROMs inside the Arduinos have a life cycle of 100,000 reads/writes. It may seem a lot, but it isn't. Only use the EEPROM when strictly needed.

Here we will program Arduino to record how many times we pressed a button. If the power is cut, it will still remember the last count using the EEPROM.

Getting ready

Following are the ingredients needed to execute this recipe:

▸ An Arduino Board connected to the computer via USB
▸ A push button

How to do it...

This recipe is based on the *Button with no resistor* recipe from *Chapter 3, Working with Buttons*. It uses the same hardware implementation with a different code.

The following code will read the last known button press count from the EEPROM and then, at each button press, will add one to that value and write it back to the EEPROM:

```
// Include the required EEPROM library
#include <EEPROM.h>

int count = 0; // Counter variable
int address = 9; // Address were we store the data in the EEPROM
int buttonPin = 12;

void setup(){
  // Read the last stored value of the button
  count = EEPROM.read(address);

  pinMode(buttonPin, INPUT_PULLUP);
```

```
    Serial.begin(9600);

    // Print the initial value in the EEPROM
    Serial.print("Initial value: ");
    Serial.println(count);
}

void loop(){
    // When button press is detected
    if (digitalRead(buttonPin) == LOW){
        count++; // increment counter
        // Write the count variable to the specified address.
        EEPROM.write(address, count % 256);
        Serial.println(count);
        delay(500); // Some debouncing delay.
    }
}
```

How it works...

The microcontroller on each Arduino has a small internal EEPROM designed to hold data even when no power is applied. The size available varies depending on the microcontroller used. For example, the Arduino Uno that uses the ATMega 328 has 1 KB, while the ATMega2560 found in the Arduino Mega2560 has 4 KB. This means that an Arduino Uno has 1,024 addresses with 1 byte each. In the code breakdown, we will explore how to use the EEPROM and the EEPROM library.

Code breakdown

As always, we need to include the EEPROM.h library:

```
#include <EEPROM.h>
```

The first function we use in the EEPROM library is the following:

```
count = EEPROM.read(address);
```

Here, we read the value found in the EEPROM at that specified address, and store it in our count variable. We do this in the setup() function so that we can begin counting at the last saved value.

Following this, we detect each time the button is pressed. When we detect that, we increment the counter and write the latest value to the same address on the EEPROM:

```
EEPROM.write(address, count % 256);
```

The EEPROM is made out of 1-byte cells, so we cannot write a number greater than 255 without overflowing. We can use multiple bytes to store larger values, but in this case, as it's just a simple demonstration, we use `count % 256` to safely start from 0 when 255 is passed.

Timing Arduino code

This is a quick and very helpful recipe. There are several time-sensitive applications on the Arduino, and sometimes we need to find the speed at which the Arduino executes various commands. Here we have a simple implementation that will tell us how much time it takes to set a digital pin at HIGH and LOW 10,000 times.

Getting ready

For this recipe, we require an Arduino board connected to a computer via USB.

How to do it...

We just need to write the following code:

```
// Variable to hold the passed time
unsigned long time = 0;
int pin = 3; // Declare a pin

void setup(){
  Serial.begin(115200); // High speed Serial
  pinMode(pin, OUTPUT);
}

void loop(){
  // Get current time
  time = micros();

  // Code to be tested for execution time
  for (int i = 0; i< 10000; i++){
    digitalWrite(pin, HIGH);
    digitalWrite(pin, LOW);
  }
  // Find the passed time and print it
  Serial.println(micros() - time);
}
```

How it works...

The `micros()` function returns the number of microseconds passed since the Arduino was turned on. Remember, there are 1,000 microseconds in a millisecond and 1,000,000 microseconds in one second.

The code simply works by recording the time before the function we want to time and after. Then, it subtracts the two and obtains the time passed. Indeed, we will also record the time it takes to make the subtraction, so the method is not perfect. However, we can determine how long it takes to make that subtraction by repeating it 10,000 times and recording the time.

External interrupts

Interrupts are weird things in the Arduino world; however, they are immensely useful. So what are they? Interrupts signal to the microcontroller that something has happened and it needs to take some action. Basically they work like this: we can attach an interrupt to a digital pin. Whenever it detects a change, it will pause anything the microcontroller is doing, execute a function we tell it to execute, and then resume normal operation.

In this example, we will fade two LEDs using PWM and while that is happening, we will be able to select which LED is fading using the button connected to an interrupt.

Getting ready

Following are the ingredients needed for this recipe:

- An Arduino board connected to a computer via USB
- Jumper cables and a breadboard
- Two standard LEDs
- Two resistors between 220–1,000 ohm
- A push button

How to do it...

The following are the steps to connect the two LEDs and the button:

1. Connect the two LEDs to the breadboard and connect their negative terminals together and to **GND**.
2. Connect to each positive LED terminal one resistor and connect the other terminal to pin 5 and pin 6.
3. Connect one terminal of the push button to GND and the other one to pin 3, which is internally connected to interrupt 1.

Schematic

Here is one possible implementation using pins 3, 5, and 6:

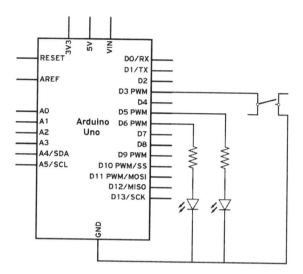

Here is a possible breadboard implementation:

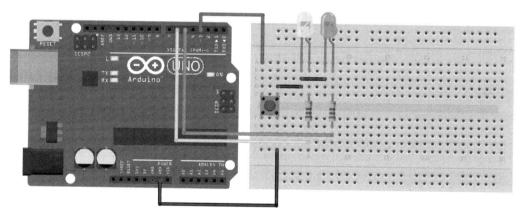

fritzing

Code

The following code will fade one external LED. When we press the button, it will change which LED is fading:

```
// Include the required Wire library for I2C
int LED1 = 5;
int LED2 = 6;

// Set a variable which we can change in the interrupt function
volatile int currentLED = LED1;

void setup(){
  // Set the button pin as an input with PULL UP resistor
  pinMode(3, INPUT_PULLUP);
  // Attach an interrupt to that pin which corresponds to interrupt 1
  // It will trigger when the input signals is FALLING
  attachInterrupt(1, changeLED, FALLING);
}

// Function that is being triggered by the interrupt
void changeLED(){
  if (currentLED == LED1) currentLED = LED2;
  else currentLED = LED1;
}

void loop(){
  // Fade In
  for (int i = 0; i < 256; i++){
    analogWrite(currentLED, i);
    delay(10);
  }

  // Fade In
  for (int i = 255; i > 0; i--){
    analogWrite(currentLED, i);
    delay(10);
  }
}
```

 Due to bouncing of the button when we press it, the interrupt might trigger several times and unexpected behavior might occur.

How it works...

When a change is detected on an interrupt pin, the code is paused, the specified function is run, and the code execution is resumed. The change can be a falling or rising edge, and a few more things. Take a look at the *There's more...* section of this recipe.

Let's look in the code breakdown.

Code breakdown

The first important difference we see is the volatile variable type:

```
volatile int currentLED = LED1;
```

The volatile variable type is a directive to the compiler. It tells to store the variable in easily accessible RAM as it will be accessed during execution. Any variable we change during an interrupt-attached function has to be volatile, otherwise weird things will happen.

In the `setup()` function, we attach a function to interrupt 1. We call the `changeLED()` function and it will trigger when there is a falling edge in the signal on the interrupt pin. For more about trigger types, take a look at the *There's more...* section of this recipe.

```
attachInterrupt(1, changeLED, FALLING);
```

Now let's explore the `changeLED` function. Any function attached to an interrupt cannot return anything (it has to be a `void` function) and cannot have any arguments. Any variable modified inside an attached function has to be volatile.

```
void changeLED(){
  if (currentLED == LED1) currentLED = LED2;
  else currentLED = LED1;
}
```

In this function, we invert the current value of the `currentLED` variable. If it's `LED1` it becomes `LED2` and so on. This function can execute at any time a `FALLING` edge is detected on the interrupt pin.

There's more...

Here we will look a little more deeply into the different things interrupts can do.

Interrupts on various Arduinos

Different Arduinos have a different amount of external interrupts. Remember, in the `attachInterrupt()` function, the first parameter is the number of the interrupt, not the digital pin on which it can be found. The following table is a good reference:

Board	Interrupt 0	Interrupt 1	Interrupt 2	Interrupt 3	Interrupt 4	Interrupt 5
Uno, Pro Mini	2	3	-	-	-	-
Mega2560	2	3	21	20	19	18
Leonardo	3	2	0	1	7	-
Yún	3	2	0	1	7	

On the Yún, pins 0 and 1 are also used for serial communication, so try to avoid them.

The Arduino Due, however, is an exception. We can assign an interrupt to any digital pin. In the `attachInterrupt` function, the first argument will actually be `digitalPin` we want to use.

About interrupt-attached functions

Remember that the code pauses when an interrupt is detected and our function is executed. Because of timer interference, the `delay()` function will not work. Also, characters received by the serial during the execution of our interrupt function might be dropped. However, the `delayMicrosecond()` function should work just fine.

In general, functions triggered by interrupt should be as short as possible with minimum impact and execution time. Otherwise, they might just do very strange things.

Different triggering modes

The last argument of the `attachInterrupt()` function is the triggering mode. There are four different modes with a fifth custom mode for the Arduino Due:

- **LOW**: This triggers the function whenever the value on the interrupt pin is LOW. If the function finishes execution and the pin is still LOW, it will execute again and again until the pin is HIGH.

- **CHANGE**: This triggers the function whenever a change is detected on the interrupt pin. Change means that either the pin switches from LOW to HIGH or from HIGH to LOW.

- **RISING**: This will trigger the function whenever the signal on the interrupt pin changes from LOW to HIGH.

▸ **FALLING**: This will trigger the function whenever the signal on the interrupt pin changes from HIGH to LOW.

▸ **HIGH**: This is a Due exclusive and works exactly like LOW mode, except that it triggers when the signal is HIGH.

Detaching an interrupt

There is also a function that detaches interrupts:

```
detachInterrupt(interrupt);
```

It requires the interrupt number as the argument. On the Due, it requires the pin number to which the interrupt was attached.

Once the detachInterrupt() function is used, a different function can be attached using the attachInterrupt() function.

Electronics – the Basics

The Arduino is an electronic platform. In order to use it properly, we need to know at least some basics about electronics, such as:

- ▶ Working of electric current
- ▶ Ohm's law
- ▶ Diodes and LEDs
- ▶ Working with breadboards

Working of electric current

Here, we will explore how electric current works. Electric current represents the flow of electrical charge in a conductor and it's measured in amperes, symbolized by A. Voltage represents the difference in electrical potential between two points of a circuit. It is measured in volts, symbolized by V. Let's think of a battery. Each battery can be considered a voltage source, and it has two terminals, a positive (+) and a negative (-). Following is one of the standardized symbols for voltage sources:

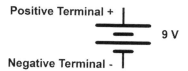

In the diagram, we see a voltage source that produces 9 volts. This means that the positive terminal has a 9 V difference over the negative terminal. The negative terminal is usually referred to as ground, GND for short. An important convention when dealing with current is the direction of current flow—from higher potential (voltage) to lower. The following diagram shows how the current flows from the positive terminal, through a resistor, back to the negative terminal:

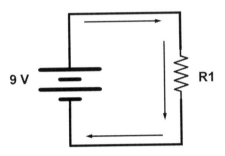

Resistance is the measure of the property of a material to oppose current flow. It's measured in ohms, symbolized by the Greek letter Ω. The resistor is the component that uses its internal resistance to restrict current flow. This is the schematic symbol, and next to it, a normal resistor:

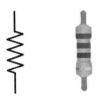

In the following section, we will see how resistors function in a circuit.

Ohm's law

Electronics is all related to Ohm's law. This provides the relation between voltage, current, and resistance in a circuit. The law states that the current passing through a resistor is directly proportional to the applied voltage across it. In mathematical forms, it looks like this:

$$I\left(current\right) = \frac{V\left(voltage\right)}{R\left(resistance\right)}$$

A simple way to remember and apply it according to either of the variables is the following triangle:

If we want to find the current, we cover **I** and we get **V** divided by **R**. The same goes for R: we cover it and we obtain V divided by I. Lastly, V will equal I multiplied with R. Let's now apply this knowledge to the following circuit:

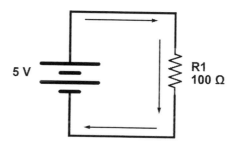

Here, we have one 5-volt voltage source in series with one resistor R1 with a resistance of 100 Ω. Because we have only one resistor, the total voltage across it will be equal to the voltage of the source, 5 V. We can now apply Ohm's law to find the current in the circuit:

$$I = \frac{V}{R} = \frac{(5V)}{100\Omega} = 0.05\,A = 50\,mA\,(milliamperes)$$

Remember that 1 ampere equals 1,000 milliamperes, represented by the unit mA.

Resistor configurations

If we have more than one resistor in series, we can use the rule of series resistance. It states that any number of resistors in series can be replaced by only one, with the resistance equal to the sum of all replaced resistances. Mathematically, it is depicted as seen here:

$$R_{series} = R_1 + R_2 + \cdots + R_n$$

The following diagram shows the two resistors on the left in series **R1** and **R2**. On the right, it shows the same circuit, but now with an equivalent resistor **R3**, which equals R1 + R2.

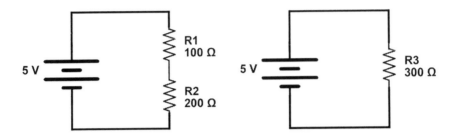

There is also the parallel resistor configuration. When we mount two or more resistors in parallel, the current is split among them. This results in a lower overall resistance. For two resistors, the formula looks like this:

$$R_{parallel} = \frac{R1 * R2}{R1 + R2}$$

The following diagram proves just that. On the left we have the normal circuit with two resistors in parallel, and on the right we have the equivalent resistor value:

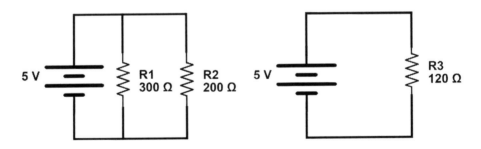

We can buy resistors with a variety of internal resistances. To easily determine what resistance a resistor has, a color code has been created. We can find the color stripes on every resistor. This is a helper diagram, which shows how to read the resistor color code:

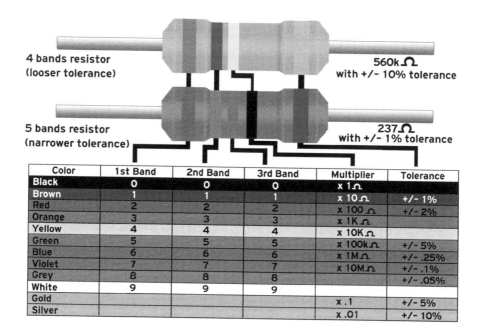

Color	1st Band	2nd Band	3rd Band	Multiplier	Tolerance
Black	0	0	0	x 1Ω	
Brown	1	1	1	x 10Ω	+/- 1%
Red	2	2	2	x 100 Ω	+/- 2%
Orange	3	3	3	x 1K Ω	
Yellow	4	4	4	x 10K Ω	
Green	5	5	5	x 100k Ω	+/- 5%
Blue	6	6	6	x 1M Ω	+/- .25%
Violet	7	7	7	x 10M Ω	+/- .1%
Grey	8	8	8		+/- .05%
White	9	9	9		
Gold				x .1	+/- 5%
Silver				x .01	+/- 10%

You can find an online equivalent resistance calculator at `http://calculator.`
`tutorvista.com/equivalent-resistance-calculator.html`.

Diodes and LEDs

There are two more components we should discuss: diodes and LEDs.

Diodes

A diode is a component that only allows current to pass in one direction. The arrow in the circuit symbol indicates this direction:

Next to the circuit symbol on the left, we have a real diode. The stripe represents the stripe in the circuit symbol, and the direction where the current goes out of the diode.

If we look at the following circuits, the one on the left will conduct current while the one on the right will not:

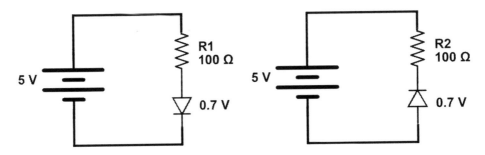

However, even when a diode allows current to pass, it drops the voltage. For a typical value, it drops the voltage by 0.7 V. Let's try and apply Ohm's law to the left circuit again. If the diode drops the voltage by 0.7 V, it means we have 4.3 V across the resistor. This will result in:

$$I = \frac{V}{R} = \frac{4.3V}{100\,\Omega} = 43\,mA$$

LEDs

There is a variation of the normal diode, called Light Emitting Diode or LED. It's basically a very small and efficient light bulb. We can find LEDs in everything these days: displays, phones, computers, toys, and so on. They have the same function as a diode, except that they also emit light when current passes through them. The electrical symbol is almost the same, but it looks completely different in real life:

They come in a variety of colors and power ratings. A typical 3-mm green LED will consume around 20 mA and will cause a 1.9 V drop across it. A diode doesn't restrict the amount of current through it, so we should always connect a resistor in series with a diode or LED. In the following schematic, we have a 20 mA LED that causes a 1.9 V drop. Let's try to calculate the perfect resistance for it:

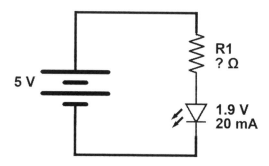

Due to the 1.9-volt drop across the LED, we only have 3.1 V across the resistor. Now we can apply Ohm's law to find the resistance:

$$R = \frac{V}{I} = \frac{3.1\,V}{20\,mA} = 155\,\Omega$$

You can find an online LED resistance calculator at `http://www.hebeiltd.com.cn/?p=zz.led.resistor.calculator`.

Working with breadboards

When we need to test a schematic, we can quickly assemble electronic components on a breadboard. It is a simple and very powerful invention that makes electronics prototyping easy.

Look at the breadboard and correlate with the following diagram. Breadboards differ in size, shape, and color but they all share the same principle:

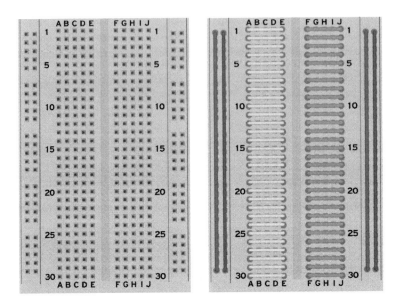

On the left we have a simple breadboard; on the right, we have the same breadboard with the internal connections shown. At the bottom and the top of the board we can see letters. If we follow, we can see that, on each row, the letters **A**, **B**, **C**, **D**, and **E** are interconnected, as shown by the yellow wire.

This means that, if we plug a pin in A, we will have a connection to B, C, D and E on the same row. Rows are not interconnected. As seen in the diagram, each row is individual. Also, on the same row, A, B, C, D, and E are not connected in any way to F, G, H, I, and J.

Some breadboards also have long power connectors on the sides. We can see them in this example by the red and black cable. These long strips are very useful for supplying power and GND to different parts of the board easily.

Index

Symbol

7-segment display
about 35
common anode (+) 40
common cathode (-) 40
connecting, to Arduino 35-39
dot 40
variations 40

A

accelerometer
about 92
connecting 92-94
URL 96
using 92
working 95
analogReadResolution() function
references 76
Analog reference (AREF) 75
Analog-to-Digital Converter (ADC) 74
analogWrite() function 117
Arduino
about 1
button 41
code basics 7
code, uploading 6, 7
code, timing 201, 202
connecting 4
connecting, to Mac OS X 5
connecting, to Windows 5
controlling, over serial 164, 166
NPN transistor, used for connecting external
load 147-150
optocouplers/optoisolators, connecting
to 154, 155

pins 9, 10
software, downloading 2-4
speaker, connecting to 143-147
tutorial, URL 180
URL 2
values, transmitting to 167
Arduino C 8, 9
Arduino Due
about 75
references 76
Arduino Mega 167
ASCII table
URL 167
attachInterrupt() function 206

B

Battery Elimination Circuit (BEC) 139
bipolar stepper motor
about 135
connecting 135-137
breadboards
working with 215, 216
brushless motors
about 138
connecting 138, 139
URL 140
working 140
bubble sort algorithm
URL 91
button
about 41
connecting 41-45
connecting, to serial 55- 57
debouncing 57-60
maintained buttons 42

Thank you for buying
Arduino Development Cookbook

About Packt Publishing

Packt, pronounced 'packed', published its first book, *Mastering phpMyAdmin for Effective MySQL Management*, in April 2004, and subsequently continued to specialize in publishing highly focused books on specific technologies and solutions.

Our books and publications share the experiences of your fellow IT professionals in adapting and customizing today's systems, applications, and frameworks. Our solution-based books give you the knowledge and power to customize the software and technologies you're using to get the job done. Packt books are more specific and less general than the IT books you have seen in the past. Our unique business model allows us to bring you more focused information, giving you more of what you need to know, and less of what you don't.

Packt is a modern yet unique publishing company that focuses on producing quality, cutting-edge books for communities of developers, administrators, and newbies alike. For more information, please visit our website at www.packtpub.com.

About Packt Open Source

In 2010, Packt launched two new brands, Packt Open Source and Packt Enterprise, in order to continue its focus on specialization. This book is part of the Packt open source brand, home to books published on software built around open source licenses, and offering information to anybody from advanced developers to budding web designers. The Open Source brand also runs Packt's open source Royalty Scheme, by which Packt gives a royalty to each open source project about whose software a book is sold.

Writing for Packt

We welcome all inquiries from people who are interested in authoring. Book proposals should be sent to author@packtpub.com. If your book idea is still at an early stage and you would like to discuss it first before writing a formal book proposal, then please contact us; one of our commissioning editors will get in touch with you.

We're not just looking for published authors; if you have strong technical skills but no writing experience, our experienced editors can help you develop a writing career, or simply get some additional reward for your expertise.

Arduino Networking

ISBN: 978-1-78398-686-6 Paperback: 118 pages

Connect your projects to the Web using the Arduino Ethernet library

1. Learn to use the Arduino Ethernet shield and Ethernet library.

2. Control the Arduino projects from your computer using the Arduino Ethernet.

3. This is a step-by-step guide to creating Internet of Things projects using the Arduino Ethernet shield.

Arduino Robotic Projects

ISBN: 978-1-78398-982-9 Paperback: 240 pages

Build awesome and complex robots with the power of Arduino

1. Develop a series of exciting robots that can sail, go under water, and fly.

2. Simple, easy-to-understand instructions to program Arduino.

3. Effectively control the movements of all types of motors using Arduino.

4. Use sensors, GSP, and a magnetic compass to give your robot direction and make it lifelike.

Please check **www.PacktPub.com** for information on our titles

Arduino Home Automation Projects

ISBN: 978-1-78398-606-4   Paperback: 132 pages

Automate your home using the powerful Arduino platform

1. Interface home automation components with Arduino.

2. Automate your projects to communicate wirelessly using XBee, Bluetooth and WiFi.

3. Build seven exciting, instruction-based home automation projects with Arduino in no time.

Internet of Things with the Arduino Yún

ISBN: 978-1-78328-800-7   Paperback: 112 pages

Projects to help you build a world of smarter things

1. Learn how to interface various sensors and actuators to the Arduino Yún and send this data in the cloud.

2. Explore the possibilities offered by the Internet of Things by using the Arduino Yún to upload measurements to Google Docs, upload pictures to Dropbox, and send live video streams to YouTube.

Please check **www.PacktPub.com** for information on our titles

66186314R00137

Made in the USA
Lexington, KY
06 August 2017